I0765583

WHEN LOVE LEARNS THE WAY BACK HOME

A Father And Son's Path Through Silence And Forgiveness

Written By:

Nicholas J. Matyas

"Every life carries a quiet wisdom. We discover it not by rushing forward, but by listening closely to where we already stand."

- Santiago Dagon

The Discovery Walkabout Collection of Reflective Writings

When Love Learns the Way Back Home

A Father and Son's Path Through Silence and Forgiveness

© 2026 Nicholas J Matyas

All rights reserved. No part of this book may be reproduced, stored in a retrieval system, or transmitted in any form or by any means electronic, mechanical, photocopying, recording, or otherwise without the prior written permission of the publisher, except for brief quotations used in reviews or scholarly works.

Santiago Dagon quotations are used with permission from Discovery Walkabout Press, as part of The Discovery Walkabout Collection of Reflective Writings.

This book is a work of reflection. It blends fact and fiction. The names, characters, dialogues, events, and examples are presented for illustrative purposes only. Any resemblance to real persons, living or deceased, is coincidental or used respectfully in service of the story's truth.

Library of Congress Control Number:
Paperback ISBN: 979-8-9936444-2-4
E-Book ISBN: 979-8-9936444-6-2

First Edition 2026
Cover design and layout by Discovery Walkabout Studio
Published by Discovery Walkabout Press
Printed in the United States of America

For permission requests, inquiries, information about educational licensing, collaborations, events, or reprint rights, contact: Discovery Walkabout Press https://discoverywalkabout.com

CONTENTS

DEDICATION

To every father who loved in silence, and every son who mistook that silence for absence.

To the men who built their affection out of action, who fixed, provided, endured, not because they lacked love, but because they did not know another way to show it.

And to the sons who, years later, finally began to see what those quiet gestures really meant.

To those who are still learning how to speak before time takes the chance away.

May these pages be a bridge between generations, between strength and tenderness, between what was felt and what was finally said.

May they remind us that love does not vanish when it goes unspoken; it only waits for courage to give it voice.

If you still have time - use it.

Listen deeply.

Speak gently.

Forgive freely.

"Speak the words while you can," Santiago Dagon wrote. **"Tomorrow may remember, but only today truly listens."**

INTRODUCTION

"Between every father and son lies a bridge made of memory and mercy. Some spend a lifetime trying to cross it; others build it with their final breath."- *Santiago Dagon*

The story of Jack and Justin is not theirs alone. It belongs to every father and son who has ever stood in the quiet space between love and misunderstanding. It belongs to generations who have carried affection like a secret, passing it forward through gestures, through endurance, through the quiet hope that effort might speak where words could not.

Jack, the father, came of age in a time when silence was safety. His world measured strength by how well a man could endure without breaking. He learned to work before he learned to speak of his feelings, and by the time he wanted to, the habit of silence had already become its own language.

Justin, the son, grew up with a different kind of noise, one filled with questions, with constant expression, with the search for meaning that his father never had the freedom to pursue. He learned to speak about everything but sometimes forgot how to listen.

Between them stretches the familiar distance of decades: one built from survival, the other from self-discovery. Both right in their own way, both lonely in their truth.

This book began as a story I have experienced and seen often, but it grew into something more: a reflection, a confession, a quiet reconciliation between two generations trying to understand what love really asks of them. Writing this book required confronting places people usually steer clear of; into the regret that lingers too long, the pride mistaken for strength, and the forgiveness that we hope arrives before it is too late.

Each page carries something lived, not just by me, but by all of us who have tried to bridge that unspoken distance between parent and child. There were days the writing felt like reopening an old wound, and others when it felt like sitting in sunlight after years of shadow.

Fathers and sons have always wrestled with time and how to express affection before it turns into apology, with how to see one another as equals before life runs out of chances. We are taught to love through instruction, not by example. And yet, somewhere in that quiet struggle lies the truth that neither strength nor vulnerability belongs to one generation alone.

If this story offers anything, let it be this: that we might all learn to pause, not to analyze, not to argue, but to listen. To see that behind every hardened exterior is a tenderness that was once afraid to speak; to realize that every silence, however heavy, was once an attempt to love in the only way someone knew how.

Love does not need to be eloquent to endure. It only needs to be present. It asks not for agreement, but for willingness to sit, to hear, to stay.

To the fathers who gave more than they ever said, and to the sons who are still trying to understand what that meant, this book is for you.

May you find, in these pages, a reflection of your own unfinished conversations. May it remind you that forgiveness is not weakness, and that love, even when imperfect, remains the most faithful echo between generations.

"The heart's great lesson," Santiago Dagon wrote, **"is that understanding is not born from agreement, but from the quiet courage to stay."**

Nicholas J Matyas

PART I

THE DISTANCE BETWEEN US

CHAPTER 1

THE BIRTH OF TWO WORLDS

"Every father was once a son trying to understand his own father."- *Santiago Dagon*

1953. The year my father was born. The world was learning how to breathe again after World War II and the Korean War.

He entered a country full of restlessness and hope, where men smoked in quiet pride and women restored order with patience. His name was Jack.

He grew into a dreamer who used his hands because life demanded work more than wonder. The world taught him that a steady job could feed a family better than a sketchbook. Still, somewhere inside him the boy with a pencil kept drawing.

When I arrived in 1991, the world had already traded silence for noise. He was born beneath the hum of factories, I beneath the glow of screens. And between those skies our voices never quite learned to meet.

Jack's childhood was built on chores, church, and discipline. He mowed lawns, painted fences, and fixed things before they broke. His father, a World War II veteran, spoke little but carried authority in the set of his jaw. Jack learned that stillness could rule a household. He told me once that the only time he saw his father cry was when their dog died. That single tear became his education in manhood.

A man provides. A man survives. A man endures pain without words.

He came of age when rebellion was measured in hair length and protest songs. He called the sixties the years when music tried to heal what politics had broken. He was not drafted for Vietnam. He said it was luck, but fate spared him because he was built for imagination, not killing.

He tried college, fell in love with a woman who looked like sunlight after rain, and Jack became my mother's husband. Neither of them yet knew that love demands more than feeling; it demands endurance.

"The young love quickly," Santiago wrote, **"because they have not yet learned the cost of patience."**

Jack painted for a time, then built furniture, then homes. Money was thin, dreams thinner. When I ask why he stopped chasing what he loved, he says, "You will understand one day. Survival has its own gravity."

He never used words like regret or failure. Yet I saw them in his silence, in the way he drove toward horizons that never came closer.

By the time I learned to walk, he had already become a man trying to keep pace with a world that no longer waited. The television became his window; the computer became mine. He searched for something real while I escaped into something virtual.

He came home tired, smelling of sour dirt and resinous sawdust. He ate fast, read the newspaper, and nodded while Mom spoke of bills and neighbors. I sat nearby, drawing spaceships, hoping for his glance. Sometimes he looked, sometimes not. That was the beginning of our quiet distance - a small misunderstanding that hardened over years.

He raised me as he was raised. Respect your elders. Work hard. Speak little. But I was a child of Why. Why work so hard for so little joy? Why not tell Mom she was beautiful? Why not hug me just because?

He said, "Life is not about feeling good. It is about doing good." I wanted warmth; he offered wisdom. He taught strength; I craved softness.

"We inherit our parents' unfinished tenderness," Santiago said. **"That's why we spend half our lives searching for what they meant to say."**

Jack was not unkind. He was untrained in tenderness. His father had loved through duty, not affection, and Jack copied the pattern. In our house, love was proof: a full fridge, a fixed bike, a paid bill. But the heart does not measure love in chores; it measures it in words left unsaid.

When I turned ten, the laughter between my parents thinned. He worked longer hours; she filled the silence with criticism. I did not know the word estrangement, but I lived inside it.

He spent evenings in the garage building things no one needed: birdhouses, small tables, excuses for solitude. I would stand in the doorway watching him sand a piece of pine beneath a single bulb. The rhythm of his hands was prayer.

Meanwhile, my own prayers happened through headphones: digital voices, video games, and endless noise. I mistook distraction for belonging.

Sometimes he asked me to help. I sighed, dragged my feet, pretended to be busy. He did not understand my world; I did not understand his. We loved each other in parallel lines, close enough to cast shadows but never touch.

"Generations do not divide," Santiago wrote. **"They echo."**

I was searching for freedom. He was searching for peace. Both of us mistook movement for meaning.

Jack's measure of worth was work. Mine was attention. He wanted stability; I wanted recognition. The same longing wore different masks.

He told stories about his father listening to the radio while carving wood. "He didn't talk much," Dad would say, smiling. "Guess I got that from him." The silence had lineage. It passed like heirloom furniture, polished but heavy.

When I was a teenager, the disagreements began. I wanted to play music; he wanted me to plan. When he said responsibility, I heard restriction. When I said freedom, he heard failure. We were not enemies. We were mistranslations of love.

If I could return to those years, I would tell him I did not need perfection, only presence. But you cannot revise childhood; you can only annotate it later.

After the divorce I found his old notebook. Inside were pencil sketches of trees and faces, drawn with hesitant grace. At the bottom of one page, he had written: Maybe someday I'll have time again. That line cut through decades. He had spent a lifetime working for hours he never owned, while I wasted mine fleeing the ones I had.

"Fathers give their sons two things," Santiago said, **"the world as it is, and the wish that it was kinder."**

We were not from different planets: only different seasons. He believed love was duty; I believed it was freedom. Now I know love is both: the duty to care, the freedom to feel.

Whenever I smell sawdust, I remember him at that workbench; the light, the quiet, the patience that was his prayer. He is older now, slower. I listen more. The words between us are fewer but truer.

We were born into two worlds, one analog, one digital, yet both longing for the same thing: to be known, to be loved, to be understood.

"Each generation teaches what the last forgot," Santiago reminds us. **"And the lesson is always the same: speak love before silence learns your name."**

CHAPTER 2

THE BREAKING POINT

"Betrayal begins in small silences." - *Santiago Dagon*

The year the house began to change, I was young enough to know feelings but not fully understand them. Old enough to hear the shift in voices, too young to know what it meant.

My mother's laughter took on a new edge, like she was laughing at a secret. My father's footsteps grew heavier. Dinner, once predictable, became a ceremony of silence. Forks touched plates. Eyes avoided each other. Words shrank to fine and good.

I did not yet know the word betrayal. I only knew that love had a sound once, and it was getting quieter.

"When adults lie," Santiago wrote, **"children inherit confusion."**

It began with a credit card bill my father did not recognize. I was on the floor with my toys when the voices rose from the kitchen. His tone was calm, hers sharp. He asked where the money went. "Don't you trust me?" she said. He did not answer.

That night he slept on the couch. The next morning, he smiled and said he had hurt his back. I knew that was not true, but it was easier to believe the lie than ask why it existed.

Soon I heard a man's name on the phone. It was not his. The air in the house shifted after that. The kind of shift you feel before a storm.

She started going out more "errands," she said. He pretended not to notice. Sometimes love does not close its eyes; it just refuses to open them.

At night I lay awake listening. Doors. Footsteps. The quiet collapse of certainty.

One evening he asked if I wanted to help him in the garage. I followed him out, even though I did not want to. He handed me sandpaper and said, "Smooth the edges." We worked side by side without speaking. After a while he stopped, wiped his brow, and looked at me. "You know I love you, right?" I nodded.

He smiled, but the smile didn't stay. Later I saw him in the truck, staring at nothing. I almost went to him, but something held me back. Maybe fear. Maybe, it was something I did not understand yet.

"Some truths arrive too soon for the heart to bear."

- Santiago Dagon

The day it all came out, I was home. He walked in holding an envelope. His hands were trembling. "Who is he?" he asked. Mom froze. The silence that followed was heavier than any shout. Then came the voices - raw, wounded, exhausted. "You never listen to me." "I've been trying to keep this family together."

I hid behind the hallway wall, covering my ears. But you cannot unhear the sound of love breaking.

When it was over, she passed me without a word. He sat at the table. His hands shook. He looked smaller, as if the air had taken something from him.

That night he slept in the truck. By morning he was gone. Mom said he needed space. I didn't know space could hurt.

For weeks, the house carried the echo of him: the clatter of dishes, the hum of the refrigerator, the door that opened and closed but did not belong to him anymore.

"Children don't break when families do," Santiago said. **"They bend, and keep bending, until they forget what straight ever felt like."**

Mom tried to make things gentle. Pancakes on Saturdays. Soft smiles. But kindness mixed with guilt tastes strange. I could feel the difference.

When Dad came back, he moved through the house like a guest. They spoke only about bills or me. They did not fight anymore, but the peace was cold.

He asked about school, about my friends. His eyes looked older. He realized words could not fix the damage that silence had caused.

I began to feel responsible for his sadness. Children do that. They think everything broken is their fault. So, I became the quiet son. Good grades, polite answers. But love that hides behind performance can't breathe.

One evening I heard them talking again. She wanted to leave. He said he could not stop her. No shouting this time. The next day she packed.

She hugged me and said, "It's not your fault." But her eyes avoided mine. Then she was gone.

He stood in the doorway for a long time. When he finally closed it, he whispered, "I don't know how to do this anymore." He was not talking to me, but I answered. "Me neither, Dad."

After that, the house settled into its new rhythm. Meals short, conversations shorter. He worked, came home, watched TV, and fell asleep in his chair. I disappeared into games and screens. It was easier to live in pixels than in silence.

"A broken home doesn't stop echoing," Santiago wrote. **"It just changes rooms."**

At school I smiled when people asked how my parents were. "They're fine." "Yeah, I'm good." Pretending became my second language.

Dad tried to fix things the way he knew, with his hands. He bought me a bike. I rode it everywhere, pedaling through guilt and confusion, pretending speed could erase what memory kept.

He once said, "Some things can't be fixed, son. You just have to work around them." I nodded, wondering if I was one of those things.

The affair was never spoken of again. Mom remarried. Dad did not. He dated a few women, but none stayed long. A part of him never came back from that night.

The fracture between us was not only about her. It was about trust. His in her. Mine in the world.

Sometimes I still see him in my memory, sitting at that table with the envelope, hands trembling. I wish I had gone to him. I wish I had said something. But children think love is indestructible until they see it bleed.

Years later I asked him why he stayed married as long as he did. "Because I still believed in her," he said. Then softer, "I didn't know how to stop believing."

Maybe that is what love really is, a kind of faith that keeps breathing even after the body of it dies.

"Forgiveness begins not when pain ends," Santiago wrote, **"but when we stop needing someone else to hurt for what they did."**

Dad never hated her. He hated himself for not being enough. And I inherited that same quiet wound. The view that love must be earned through suffering.

The breaking point was not the affair. It was the silence that followed. The distance that grew not from anger but from fatigue.

He still signed every birthday card Love, Dad. I still said Love you too. The words remained, but they had changed shape. They were not promises anymore. They were reminders that once, before the silence, we believed in something that could hold.

"Even the strongest heart can fracture under the weight of what's unsaid," Santiago Dagon wrote. **"And still, somehow, it keeps beating."**

CHAPTER 3

THE HOUSE DIVIDED

"Children of divorce become translators of two worlds."

- Santiago Dagon

Two Homes, Two Rules

The divorce arrived without shouting. No slammed doors. No neighbors standing outside to listen. Just signatures, cardboard boxes, and the crisis of a family being divided into two separate places.

I was old enough to sense an ending. Too young to understand how long endings last.

Mom moved into a small duplex across town. It smelled like fresh paint and perfume, a brightness that made the rooms feel new but not yet warm. Dad stayed in the old house, the one with the creaky floors and the dent in the hallway where my toy truck had once met the wall.

Two homes. Two bedrooms. Two sets of toothbrushes lined up like little soldiers in different armies. And two versions of me.

Mom called her place a fresh start. Dad called the old place home. I lived between those sentences, with a backpack full of clothes and confusion.

At Mom's everything was new. New couch, new dishes, a new routine that sounded like order. Before long there was a new boyfriend who laughed loudly and complimented her cooking. Her smile was brighter when he was there, yet it flickered when he was not. She seemed to smile for them both, and for who she might become.

At Dad's everything stayed the same, only quieter. The furniture remembered us. The air carried sawdust and coffee. He moved slower, spoke softer, and cooked simple dinners. Canned soup. Scrambled eggs. Toast that arrived at the table with too much butter because he could not think of another way to make it feel like love.

He asked what I wanted to eat as if the right answer might fix the room. I told him anything was fine because nothing really was.

He bought a blue blanket with racing stripes to make my bed look more like mine. I thanked him. But when I pulled it up at night it felt like a flag I was expected to salute. Temporary comfort. Temporary life.

Mom's house had rules about shoes by the door and homework before screens. Dad's house had rules about please and thank you and this is how we speak in this home. Both loved me. Both believed they were right. I just wanted to stop feeling torn.

So I adapted. At Mom's I learned to be quiet when the wine bottle opened. At Dad's I learned to give him space when he stayed in the garage too long. I became fluent in tension, reading moods the way other kids read books.

"A child raised between two worlds learns survival before trust," Santiago wrote. **"And that is a hard habit to unlearn."**

At school I did not talk about it. Most children still lived under one roof. My life felt like a puzzle missing its picture on the box.

I started to feel like a visitor in both places. When I unpacked at Mom's I felt Dad watching me from a memory. When I left Dad's on Sunday night I turned back and saw him on the porch with that half wave fathers use when they hide a tear. It hurt to see him like that. I pretended it did not. Faking it was the only way I knew how to interact.

The Boy Between Parents

The split was not only legal. It was geography. Every conversation became a map I had to cross without stepping on a fault line.

Mom asked, "Did your father say anything about me?" I shook my head. I would rather carry the lie than watch that shadow pass over her face.

Dad asked, "How is your mom doing?" I said, "She is fine." I would rather swallow the truth than pull the stitches from his heart.

They spoke through me. I became the messenger, the filter, the boy who edited sentences for adult feelings. Words were given to me that were never meant for children to hold.

Sometimes Dad handed me a twenty for snacks. Mom saw it and said, "You do not need to carry his guilt." I did not know what guilt looked like. But it was heavy in my pocket.

She bought me clothes to make up for lost time. He fixed my bike to make up for what nobody could repair. Both loved me. Both were lost.

On Dad weekends we watched old westerns where men said little and did the right thing anyway. He looked over at me during those quiet scenes as if the movie might lend him a sentence. The words did not come.

At Mom's, the television was louder. Reality shows ended with hugs and tidy speeches. See, she said, people fight and then they work it out. I nodded, but the story on our couch did not match the one on the screen.

"The child of divorce becomes the peacekeeper of ghosts," Santiago wrote. **"He learns to hold love in halves, afraid that if he gives one piece away, he will lose the other."**

So, I kept small secrets. Not the reckless kind. The protective kind. Who I liked at school. What I feared at night. I hid those in the space between houses where no one could ask for them.

Every Sunday Dad drove me back. We listened to the radio. Old songs about leaving and coming home. He tapped the wheel when he wanted to speak. Tapping became his language for everything.

When we pulled up, he said, "Be good for your mom." He never said I will miss you. I heard it anyway in the pause before he drove away.

Mom met me at the door. "Did you have fun?" I nod "Yes." "What did you do?" "Just Stuff." "With whom?" "No one you know." She smiled but her eyes searched for evidence. I gave her the edited version. I learned to edit my love.

At night I lay in the dark and imagined the two houses as planets circling the same sun. I was the small satellite tugged by both, moving in a line that never let me land long enough to belong.

The Price of a Split Childhood

The cost of divorce is not only measured in money or furniture. It is the slow spending of innocence. It is the quiet education that forever does not always mean forever.

Mom got a new last name. Her new husband, David, preferred schedules, and neat lines. A boy needs discipline, he said. I had plenty. What I needed was understanding.

Dad did not speak against him. He asked, "Is he good to you?" I said "yes," though I was not sure what good meant anymore. Dad nodded and looked down, relieved and wounded at the same time. I imagined a door inside him that kept closing and opening, each time a little slower.

At Dad's nothing much changed. Work. Home. The faithful garage. He brought home a dog named Cooper and said it was for me. But I watched the way he rested his hand on that warm back. The dog was a bridge for the nights when words would not cross.

I threw the ball in the yard while Dad stood on the porch with a beer. Pride and grief shared his face. He did not know how to talk about Mom anymore. He did not know how to talk about much of anything. But he would pat my shoulder with that careful touch men use when they are trying not to say the wrong thing. Sometimes it was enough. Sometimes it was not.

At Mom's, the house was brighter, louder, cleaner. But I missed the quiet hum of Dad's place even when it ached. At Dad's I missed the warmth of Mom's house even when the warmth felt borrowed. Every Hello and See You Later became a small betrayal of the person I had just left.

"Children of separation grow into adults who apologize for existing," Santiago wrote. **"They learn early that love can be conditional, even when it should not be."**

The weekend shuttle wore me down. Friday to Sunday, out and back, like a tide with no moon to govern it. My life fit inside a duffel bag. My identity folded between jeans and T shirts.

On school forms I hesitated at the line that said address. Which one? The question did not fit in the box.

I stopped talking much. Dad asked, "If I was okay?" I said "Yes." Mom said I was moody. They blamed each other for my silence. Neither did I fully understand that my quietness had two addresses.

Other kids complained about strict parents. I envied them. A house with one set of rules is still a house.

The hardest part was not the distance. It was the pretending. Pretending I was not angry. Pretending I was not lonely. Pretending that flipping the bedroom light switch and saying goodbye were nothing more than routine. When you live in two places long enough you begin to believe that you belong in none.

When I reached the age to drive, Dad gave me an old pickup he had rebuilt himself. The paint faded. The doors were dented. The engine was steady, like a promise he could finally keep. Now you can visit me whenever you want, he said.

I thanked him and drove away. Freedom felt like escape. I did not visit as often as he hoped. Choosing is hard when every choice feels like a wound.

"We lose our parents long before they die," Santiago wrote. **"Not because they stop loving us, but because we stop knowing how to love them."**

I wish I had known that then. That divorce makes fewer villains than it makes survivors. That love does not vanish; it changes shape and waits for the heart to grow into it. But I was still learning and fluent in anger. Fluent in vanishing acts.

One afternoon Mom said, "You are just like your father." She meant it to scare me. Strangely, I felt proud. She saw it on my face and did not say it again.

That night I drove the truck to an open field outside town. I turned off the headlights and let the darkness hold me. Grass, rain, the clean breath of the earth. I thought, Maybe one day the ache will quiet. I waited. It did not.

"Home is not a place," Santiago Dagon wrote. **"It is where the ache finally quiets."**

I am still looking for that place. I believe it exists somewhere. It might be a kitchen where the coffee is shared, and no one is measuring blame. It might be a porch where a father can wave without hiding his eyes. It might be a phone call where a son does not edit his love.

Two homes. Two rules. One heart trying to learn a single language again.

CHAPTER 4

INHERITED SHADOWS

"We inherit silence as easily as we inherit blood."

- Santiago Dagon

The Grandfathers' Quiet Legacy

I did not really know my grandfathers. By the time I was old enough to ask the right questions, both had already faded into photographs and kitchen table stories. What I knew of them lived inside the men who came after them. Their presence was a hush passed down, a way of standing in a doorway, a way of swallowing a feeling before it reached the mouth.

My father spoke of his dad with a mixture of respect and fatigue. He worked, he came home, he fixed things. He did not complain, did not cry, did not explain. He had learned to survive the long hunger of the Great Depression and the hard rationing of war. When the country called, he went. When the war ended, he returned to the factory as if nothing had happened to the world or to his own heart. Forty years at the same bench, the whistle was like a bell that told him who he was.

There are no family stories about tenderness, only about his duty. No long embraces. No apologies. No space for healing. No language for innocence beyond the tightening of a jaw.

My father inherited that rhythm. He believed a man is made by his endurance. He believed a steady back and a quiet mouth could hold a family in place. And in his time, perhaps they could. Those men built houses and highways and paychecks. They laid down roads and rules. They built walls, too, but did not call them that.

"The Silent Generation and Baby Boomers taught their sons how to build worlds, not how to feel them."- *Santiago Dagon*

On my mother's side, the story rhymed with a different melody. Her father was a carpenter who drank quietly and laughed loudly and died earlier than anyone expected. He was loyal, strong, and missing in the same way many men of his time were missing. When my grandmother spoke of him, she used only two measures. He was a good man. He worked hard. That was the highest praise they knew. It meant the bills were paid and the lawn was cut and the motor turned over on cold mornings.

I have learned that good does not always mean whole. One grandfather survived a war overseas. The other survived the slow war of daily life. Their silences became the soil in which my parents grew. Their restraint shaped how they showed affection, how they argued, and how they left a room when the air was no longer friendly. It took me years to see my father's quiet as inheritance and not indifference. He did not avoid emotion because he did not care. He avoided it because it was not a tool his father had left him.

I can see it now, a table of men across decades. Each wants to say something kind. The tragedy is not that they did not love. The tragedy is that they did, and no one taught them how to show it.

The Silent Men Who Raised the Loud World

By my twenties, the world was so loud that silence felt like a relic. We carried microphones in our pockets. We shared every meal, every thought, every bruise that wanted attention. We spoke constantly and still felt unseen. Our grandfathers were raised by radio and ration books. We were raised by screens and social feeds. They fixed engines. We edited captions. They built houses. We built profiles. The ache was the same across the generations.

My father told me his dad never spoke about the war. Sometimes he would find him alone in the shed studying a photograph. When asked what he was thinking, the answer was always the same. Nothing.

But silence has weight. It gathers at the back of the throat and behind the eyes. It lives in the shoulder that never relaxes, in the hand that grips a coffee mug as if it were the only thing keeping a man from falling through the floor. My father carried that weight without knowing it had a name.

I once asked if his father ever told him he loved him. "No," he said, then smiled. "He did not have to. I knew." I did not argue, but I wondered what it costs a boy to perform that translation every day. Perhaps in those years love did not need words because presence was enough. A man came home, he stayed, he fixed what broke. That was a sentence, not a fragment. Now presence is the rare thing. We are surrounded by signals and still wait for someone to arrive.

"The world learned to speak louder but not deeper," Santiago said. **"So we built volume where our fathers built silence."**

I watched a video once of soldiers returning from deployment. They hugged their children and wept openly. It was beautiful and it confused me. I wondered what my grandfather would have felt seeing that kind of softness paraded through an airport. Would he call it weakness? Would he call it freedom? Would he have envied the permission?

The men of his time fought more than one battle. They fought in places where there were no maps to navigate and in hidden scars where family had no permission to heal. Emotion did not pay the mortgage. Emotion did not keep food on the table. Emotion did not make it through the winter. So they declared a truce with feeling and made fortresses of their sons. Strong. Silent. Resolute. Those sons became fathers who tried to hold a home together by tightening every bolt in the door. Then came sons like me, flooded with questions, hungry for connection, and uncertain how to ask for it without sounding ungrateful.

It is strange how love mutates over time. Each generation inherits what the last could not face. My father remembers his dad polishing his shoes every Sunday before church, the porch afterward, the coffee cooling in a chipped mug, the pride that never announced itself. "He never raised his voice," my father says. "He did not have to." Then he adds, softly, "I guess that is where I got it." It is not a boast. It is a confession.

What Sons Learn Without Being Told

People say children do not listen to what you say. They watch what you do. I would add one more truth. We inherit what you never say.

I did not grow up with shouting or fists. I grew up inside a quiet that sometimes pressed against my ribs. Silence, when it lasts long enough, finds a way to bruise. My father did not mean to pass it on. He was repeating a lesson he did not know he had learned. A lineage of men who tried to be stronger than their pain. A lineage that confused vulnerability with weakness and discipline with dignity.

"What we call discipline was often just fear dressed in order,"
- Santiago Dagon

When I was young, I wanted my father to talk more. Tell stories. Ask questions. Open the door and leave it open. Instead, he loved by example. He changed the oil in my car. He paid for what he could before I had to ask. At the time I called it control. Now I call it care.

He did not know how to say, "I worry about you." He said drive safe.

He did not know how to say, "I am proud of you." He said keep at it.

He did not know how to say, "I miss you." He said call when you can.

It took me years to hear the real sentences inside those smaller ones.

The grandfathers left us restraint. The fathers learned endurance. The sons received confusion. If we are fortunate, confusion matures into understanding before we hand it to our children.

Breaking a pattern is holy work. It hurts because it asks you to feel what the others could not.

It asks you to hold the family's unshed tears and name them without turning away.

I visited my grandmother once in late afternoon. We sat on her porch while the cicadas kept time. I asked her about the man she loved. "Patient," she said. "Able. Heavy when he drank." Then she added the sentence that explained every man I have known in our family. "He never knew how to rest. Even when he smiled, he was still working inside."

Always working inside. Building something no one could see. Repairing something no one could touch.

Sometimes I wonder who we would be if rest had been taught alongside duty. If softness came without shame. If apologies were not treated like surrender, but like medicine.

Would my father have hardened so quickly? Would I have stood so far away? Would love have been easier to recognize in a dark room?

I try to be fair with the past. Maybe their silence was another form of devotion. Maybe it was love in its unfinished state, still searching for its words.

"Every man carries his father's unfinished apology," Santiago wrote. **"Some spend their whole lives trying to deliver it. Others finally decide to forgive it."**

I am learning to forgive it.

For him.

For me.

Because the truth is simple and stubborn. I have also become one of them. I love deeply and speak softly. I fix it before I feel. I still measure affection with actions and receipts. And yet I am trying to place words where our fathers placed only labor. Trying to speak early, not after the door closes. Trying to let my children, or the child who will one day trust me, hear the sentence clean.

I love you. I am proud of you. You are enough.

That is how an inheritance ends and a legacy begins, allowing love and feelings in.

I found a letter once that my grandfather wrote to my father near the end of his life. Only a few lines in precise cursive. It said, I hope you are proud of the man you have become. I know I am. I wish I said it more often. My father never showed it to anyone. I found it folded into a book he had moved from house to house. The paper was soft from being opened. The crease was worn by a thumb that kept returning to the same line. He had carried those words for years, waiting for the moment he could believe them. I recognized the waiting. I do it too.

The lineage of quiet men lives in me.

So does the hope to speak differently. Healing is not a rebellion against our fathers. It is love continuing its work, finally using the language it always deserved.

"Healing is not rebellion," Santiago Dagon reminds us. **"It is the quiet continuation of love, finally spoken aloud."**

CHAPTER 5

MESSAGES UNREAD

"Love didn't vanish when we stopped writing letters, it just began to hide inside the spaces we forgot to reply to."

- Santiago Dagon

The Years of Silence

The years after college slipped into a kind of quiet, I had never known. Not the peaceful quiet of contentment, but the hollow kind; the one that hums faintly beneath every ordinary day. It is the quiet that settles between people who love each other but have forgotten how to speak.

My father and I never fought. There was no final argument, no slammed door. Just a slow drift, the kind that happens without notice. A text missed here, a call postponed there. Silence growing in the small pauses we no longer tried to fill.

It began gently, like snow gathering on windowsills.

We exchanged short, practical messages. Need anything? You good? Happy birthday.

Replies came hours later, sometimes days. Each message like a pebble skipping across water; brief, deliberate, never sinking deep.

We were both alive, both existing, but in different worlds. He still believing in paper bills, face-to-face conversations, and weather reports delivered by the same news anchor every night. I was chasing deadlines, checking updates, living through filtered blue light.

He called the bank when he needed something. I used an app. He left voicemails. I left short text messages.

Sorry Busy Now became our mutual excuse, our shared defense against vulnerability. It was easier to say I am busy than to say I'm lonely.

When I visited, we would sit at the kitchen table like two men performing politeness. He would ask if I was eating well. I would ask how his back felt. He would tell me about the neighbor's new roof. I would nod, pretending to care.

We both loved each other, but we had traded warmth for safety. Our affection lived in gestures now with him filling my gas tank before I left, me fixing his phone every time I came home.

Somewhere along the way, that quiet became comfortable. Familiar. Even kind. **"Silence between people who love each other is not always absence,"** Santiago wrote. **"But sometimes it becomes the slow rehearsal of goodbye."**

Looking back, I was not angry. I was afraid.

Afraid that talking might bring back everything we had worked so hard to bury: the broken marriage, the disappointments, the distance. So instead of speaking, we waited. Two men holding love like a fragile object, neither brave enough to unwrap it first.

Love in the Age of Notifications

Technology tricked us into believing we were close. Every time my phone lit up with his name, I felt that brief pulse of affection followed almost immediately by guilt when I did not answer.

Our relationship became a series of messages that could fit on a single screen. How's work? Busy but good. You? Fine. Just tired.

Sometimes he sent pictures of the garden. His bright shiny tomatoes lined up neatly, or the dog sleeping under the shade of a tree. His captions were simple: Look at this beautiful view.

It was his way of saying I am still here.

But I never replied with what I felt. I never typed I miss you, even when I thought it. It seemed too heavy for the clean space of a text box.

We live in a world where love now has a timestamp. Where you can see when someone reads your message, when they start typing and stop. Those three dots became our whole conversation: appearing, vanishing, returning. The digital version of hesitation.

I sent him a photo once of my new apartment. He wrote back: Nice place. Looks clean.

That was all. There was no uplifting like I am proud of you. Nor the ask for an invitation, I wish I could visit.

At first, I laughed. Later, I sat with the sting of it. He was not trying to be cold. That was just how his generation learned to love, through understatement and through restraint.

But I wanted more. I wanted his approval to sound like joy.

I almost typed I miss you, Dad, but deleted it before I could press send. I told myself he already knew.

I used to believe technology made us colder. Now, I think it simply shows how scared we are to be warm.

We replace I love you with emojis. We send hearts instead of words. We scroll past calls for help because answering means revealing we still care.

"In a world of constant communication," Santiago wrote, **"we have forgotten how to listen."**

There were nights he called and I let it ring. Not because I did not care, but because I didn't know what to say. The small talk felt useless, and the big talk felt impossible.

He would leave voicemails, short ones that made my throat tighten. "Hey son, just checking in. No rush to call back."

I would listen days later, replaying his voice. It sounded softer than I remembered, slower. Like time was catching up with him.

Sometimes I would replay them at night, alone in bed. It was the only time I let myself feel the ache. I would think about calling him back, but the thought never turned into courage.

So I would text instead.

And that became our new form of intimacy: short, efficient, always safe. A thread of messages stretching through the years, proof that we had not disappeared, but also that we had not truly connected.

What We Don't Reply To

The last time I saw him before everything changed was on a Sunday. He was on the roof, repairing shingles.

I told him to hire someone. He laughed. "I still got it." But I noticed the tremor in his hands.

Afterward we sat on the porch, lemonade between us, cicadas humming like an old clock. He asked about my life. I said "Busy." He nodded. That word had become the bridge between our two worlds: sturdy, meaningless, safe.

He asked if I had ever thought about moving back home. I said "Maybe." He looked toward the trees for a long while, then said, "Don't wait too long to make your life mean something."

I laughed, thinking it was advice about ambition. But his eyes stayed steady. He was not talking about success. He was talking about me and about us.

When I left, he hugged me longer than usual. "Proud of you, son," he said.

For a second, the world stopped. It was the first time I had heard those words spoken out loud.

I wanted to say *I'm proud of you too*, but the words caught somewhere in the throat, trapped behind the years we both stayed silent.

Driving away, I felt the ache of that unfinished sentence following me down the road.

A week later, he texted a photo of the finished roof with caption "All done. Not bad for an old man, huh?"

I smiled, typed "Looks great, Dad," but never sent it. I told myself I would reply later. I never did.

That unsent message lived in my phone for months like a digital ghost.

"Every unread message is a small confession," Santiago wrote. **"Not of neglect, but of fear that if we open it, we'll have to open ourselves too."**

When I finally visited again, the roof looked solid, clean, perfect. He had grown thinner. His steps were slower. He asked for help moving boxes. We worked in silence, each pretending it was normal. I caught him watching me once, eyes soft, like he was memorizing something.

That night, I went through our old messages. Years of half-conversations. Thanks. Ok. Love you too.

Not one of them said what we really meant. We had learned to talk like men who feared being misunderstood.

He once told me, "You are lucky. You grew up in a world where people can talk about their feelings."

He said it like a privilege. I think he was right, it was. And I wasted it.

Maybe he did not understand that silence had become my inheritance. And maybe, I did not understand that silence was how he made peace with what he could not fix.

I sometimes wonder how many fathers and sons live like this; their whole relationship suspended in drafts and half-written texts. How many sons stare at glowing screens, trying to find the courage to send one real sentence. How many fathers wait beside phones that never ring.

"We are the first generation to archive our distance," Santiago Dagon wrote. **"Screens have become our diaries, full of conversations we were too afraid to finish."**

I wish I had finished ours. But I did not know time was already running out. No one ever does until the phone rings and silence finally answers back.

PART II

THE YEARS BETWEEN WORDS

CHAPTER 6

THE SON WHO STOPPED
BELIEVING

"Faith doesn't always disappear. Sometimes it hides behind disappointment."- *Santiago Dagon*

Isolation as Survival

There comes a season when a young man stops recognizing his own life. For me, it did not arrive with alarms. It arrived like light that could not finish its work. Morning after morning, a little dimmer than before.

I was twenty five. Old enough to be spoken to like a man. Too unsure to feel like one.

My job paid the rent. My friends texted often. My apartment looked fine from the sidewalk. Inside, there was a quiet that did not bring peace. I woke tired, even after nights that were not long. I stayed up late anyway, drifting through other people's

41

days. Smiling faces. Lifted glasses. Perfect sunsets taken from perfect angles. I did not feel envy. I felt distance.

Nothing terrible had happened. That was the trouble. You can name pain when it arrives in full costume. But the slow unraveling has no headline. It only has static.

I had learned to hide my feelings earlier in life. After the divorce, quiet kept me safe. I kept it. I wore it into my twenties like a coat that did not fit but still kept the rain off.

Dad called sometimes asking, "Everything good?" "Yeah okay" I say. "Proud of you," he replies. "Thanks." I answer. We were fluent in endurance. But endurance is not living. It is a bridge you use too long because you are afraid of boats.

"Isolation begins as protection," Santiago wrote, **"but it ends as self erasure."**

One evening I stood in front of the mirror and could not make eye contact with myself. Not because I was ashamed. Because I felt like I was looking at a neighbor. The eyes were there, but the person behind them kept stepping out of frame.

People said I was thoughtful. They meant kind. I heard quiet. They said I was steady. They meant dependable. I heard drifting.

When friends invited me out, I said I was tired. Sometimes I was. Mostly I feared the weight of conversation. Every question felt like a test I was not ready to take. What have you been up to? How is work? Are you seeing anyone? I could answer all of them, yet none of my answers felt like the truth.

I was not depressed. Or maybe I was and would not name it. I was disconnected. From other people, from myself, from whatever once made a day feel like a promise.

Late at night I thought of my father's routine. Rise early. Work. Supper. Sleep. Repeat. I used to judge it. Now I envied the shape of it. Even a narrow road is a road.

Faith Lost in Noise

I did not grow up with church. Mom spoke of karma. Dad spoke of keeping your word. We bowed our heads for weddings and funerals. On ordinary Sundays we did laundry.

Still, I believed in something. Maybe not God. But goodness. The sense that life had a current. That if you swam with care, you would find yourself carried toward meaning.

That belief thinned as time went on. Good people got sick. Kind people got left. Families collapsed in houses that looked stable from the street. I began to suspect the universe was polite, not attentive.

Faith, for me, became a language I had never been taught. I recognized its music. I could not sing it.

Dad carried a small faith he never argued about. Not doctrine. Decency. He believed right work is prayer. He believed showing up is a sacred act. He fixed neighbors' steps, lent money he did not have, drove people home who lived nowhere near our street. He never quoted scripture. He kept appointments with kindness.

I admired him. I could not follow him. The world I lived in rewarded speed over sincerity. It rewarded reaction over reflection. We counted ourselves by echoes. Likes. Views. Hearts. We did not pray. We posted. We did not confess. We captioned.

"The digital world gave us every voice except our own," Santiago wrote.

I told Dad once that life felt pointless. He put his hands on the table like he was steadying it. "What do you mean?" I muttered, "Everything moves. Jobs move. People move. Even happy moves." He nodded. "Maybe that is why it matters," he said. Then, gentler, "You think too much, son."

It sounded like care and dismissal at once. Thinking too much is heavy when your thoughts have no home. There is a loneliness that comes from seeing through things early. You find the crack in the cup while everyone else is still drinking. You investigate love with a flashlight instead of a candle.

I used to believe connection could heal anything. Then connection turned fragile in my hands. So much effort for a string that kept breaking. Scroll, smile, type, send, wait. Every success story on my screen made me smaller, not because I did not cheer for them, but because I could not find my own momentum.

Faith did not slam its door. It slipped out. It left its coat on the chair to make me think it was still there. In its place came logic with sharp corners, sarcasm that made people laugh, and the quiet glare of a phone at midnight.

"Faith does not always die," Santiago said. **"It hides behind the noise."**

The Digital Refuge

When I could not locate myself in the real world, I found myself online. It was easier to be a voice than a person. Easier to be quick than to be known.

I played games late into the night. New maps. New quests. New friends I would never meet. We spoke with the easy honesty of people who would not bump into each other at the grocery store. Strategy first. Then jokes. Then life, a little at a time.

A player from Canada said something I still keep. "We are all alone together." We laughed. Then we kept playing. But the sentence stayed. That is the internet's truest shape. Shared isolation. Ten thousand lit windows. No one opening the blinds.

Dad did not understand gaming. He called and heard the clack of keys. "What are you doing up?" "Just working on a project." A small lie that protected a larger need. If I told him, I was playing he would think I was wasting time. He would not know it was the only room where my voice moved without stumbling.

"Technology does not disconnect us," Santiago wrote. "It mirrors the disconnection already there."

I was not avoiding my father. I was avoiding the version of myself who did not know what to say to him. The son who had questions he could not speak without shaking. The man who could not trust love to stay. The boy who kept the family's silence under his shirt like a scar.

Some nights I played until sunrise. The screen was my dawn. Victory screens flashed. Laughter buzzed in my headset. Then the match ended. The room remembered it was empty. It was not joy. But it was close to feeling. Close to warmth. Close enough to return to.

I began to visit less and less. "When will you visit?" he asked. "Soon," I said. Weeks turned into later. Later turned into let me try next month. He did not press. He had learned not to chase a silence that would only run faster. "Okay. Take care, son." He said wanting more.

I looked at that message longer than I want to admit. He believed I was busy. I was busy. Busy avoiding the distance by living inside a smaller one.

The digital world gave me control. Mute. Hide. Leave. Return. In real life there is no button for any of those. There is only the door, and the courage it takes to knock on it again.

When the headset was off and the room went dark, I sometimes heard his voice inside my head. Not words. The timbre of them. Low. Solid. Certain. It made me miss what I never fully had. A father I could talk to without translating myself.

Dad's faith was simple. Work. People. Persistence. Mine was distraction with a clean user interface. And yet there he was in me. In the quiet ways I stepped around my feelings. In the pride that kept me from the first apology. In the nameless ache I carried like a pocketed stone.

Maybe belief does not leave. Maybe it waits. Buried beneath noise. Waiting for a quieter room.

"The heart never stops believing," Santiago Dagon wrote. **"It just stops listening when the world grows too loud."**

I am learning to turn the volume down. One night at a time. One call at a time. One word at a time that does not try to solve anything, only to say, I am here. That is where faith begins again. Not with answers. With presence. With the courage to be heard.

CHAPTER 7

THE FATHER WHO COULDN'T LET GO

"Time softens anger, but it sharpens regret."

- Santiago Dagon

The Guilt Years

By the time Jack turned sixty, the house had grown quieter than memory. No footsteps in the hall. No music from the back room. Only the clock, steady and indifferent, marking seconds he no longer knew what to do with.

Each morning, he sat by the kitchen window with a mug of coffee warming his hands. Beyond the glass stood the oak tree he had planted the year Justin was born. It was tall now, a canopy of green that stretched across the yard. He could still remember digging that hole, sweat running down his back, thinking how one day they would sit beneath it together. They never did.

The silence between them had hardened into its own kind of presence. Not anger anymore. Not even pride. Just a slow ache that filled the rooms where voices used to live.

Jack had tried. He called. He left messages. He sent texts written carefully, as if the right wording could repair a lifetime.

Most went unanswered. When replies did come, they were short. Fine. Busy. All good.

He did not blame Justin anymore. He blamed himself for every conversation that had turned into correction, for every moment when discipline felt easier than understanding.

He could still see himself on the porch, young and impatient, speaking to his son in tones he thought were strength. Years later, he realized they were only fear, the fear of losing control, fear of raising a man softer than the world would allow.

"Regret is not born from what we do," Santiago wrote, **"but from the gentleness we withheld."**

Jack thought often about small things that had cost him more than he knew. The day Justin tried to fix his bike, and Jack snatched the wrench from his hands. The moment he said "Let me do it" when what the boy needed was "You are doing fine. "He finished the repair, handed the bike back, and went inside, never noticing how much silence followed him.

Now those moments returned like ghosts that did not want to frighten him, only to be remembered. He told himself there was still time that forgiveness, like the seasons, always returned. But as his hair silvered and his breath shortened, time began to feel like a guest overstaying its welcome.

He often wondered if love, once left unattended, could ever find its way home again.

Love in Small Gestures

Jack had never been a man of grand declarations. He came from a generation that showed love by fixing what broke. So he kept fixing things.

He repaired the loose fence board that Justin had once kicked after an argument. He kept the grass short, though no one walked across it anymore. He replaced the porch bulb every few months, telling himself it was for safety, when really it was for hope.

Every few weeks he texted: Just checking in. You doing okay?

Sometimes Justin replied. Sometimes not. When the phone stayed silent, Jack convinced himself it was fine. He knew his son was busy. Busy was a kind word for distance.

When a message did arrive, short and polite, Jack read it again and again. He searched for hidden meaning in the brevity, a softness between the lines.

He wanted to say something more than Take Care, but language felt too fragile. Words had always failed him when he needed them most.

So he sent pictures instead; the dog in the sunlight, tomatoes on the fence, snow gathering on the porch rail. He hoped Justin would see these small glimpses and remember that the world could still be gentle.

"When words fail," Santiago Dagon wrote, **"the heart turns to repetition. We keep showing love in the same way, hoping one day someone will understand the language."**

On Justin's birthday, Jack mailed a card every year. Always the same note: Proud of you. Love, Dad. Three words that felt too small, yet somehow too heavy to hold more. He slid twenty dollars inside, not because Justin needed it, but because a father needs to give something, even if it is only the symbol of care.

Late at night, Jack often sat in the living room with the television dark and the photo albums open. He traced the corners of old pictures, the ink fading but the faces alive. There was Justin, six years old, holding a fishing pole too big for his hands. There he was again, twelve, at the county fair, smiling through crooked teeth.

Jack whispered apologies into the quiet, not because he expected an answer, but because he needed to hear them out loud. He missed the sound of his son's laughter, the easy rhythm of small talk. Now when the phone rang, it was the clinic, the pharmacy, or another friend's widow calling with news that someone else was gone.

Love, he thought, had become a kind of maintenance; watering the garden, feeding the dog, keeping things alive that would wither if left alone.

He was not waiting for forgiveness anymore. He was waiting for the chance to be seen again, not as the man who failed, but as the one who kept trying.

What Fathers Never Say

The doctor told him his heart was weakening. Jack nodded and smiled like it was a weather report. He had felt the decline long before the charts confirmed it. He did not tell Justin. He told himself he would "next time," but next time was a guest that never knocked.

He began leaving small notes on the kitchen table, fragments of what he wished he had said aloud. One read: I was proud of you every day, even the days I didn't say it. Another: I'm sorry I was hard on you. I didn't know another way. And a third, folded into his wallet: Don't let my silence become yours.

He hoped one day his son might find them.

Sometimes he picked up the phone, ready to dial. But words would gather like fog shapeless, uncatchable. So he prayed instead, not for miracles, but for the patience to stay thankful. Thank you for the years, he whispered. Thank you for a son who still calls me Dad, even if only in memory.

"Fathers rarely say the things they feel," Santiago wrote. **"Not because they don't feel them, but because the words arrive too late to matter."**

In the mirror, Jack began to see his own father staring back in the same tired kindness, the same unspoken longing. He finally understood how love can hide inside silence, how pride can mask apology. One evening, he looked at his reflection and said softly, "I forgive you, Dad." Then after a long pause, "I hope he forgives me too."

He thought about writing a letter to Justin. He even began one. Dear Son,.

He stopped there. The page waited, patient and white, like all the years between them. How do you fit an entire life into one sheet of paper? How do you apologize for not knowing how to love out loud?

He folded the letter and placed it in the drawer beside his bed.

Every night he checked the porch light before going to sleep. It burned steadily, its glow stretching down the driveway. He told himself it was habit. But it was faith. A faith in the smallest form a man can hold.

Because hope, for Jack, was no longer about happy conclusions. It was the quiet courage of waiting. The belief that one day there might still be a knock at the door, or a voice calling from the yard, saying the simplest thing of all: Hey, Dad.

"The greatest courage," Santiago Dagon wrote, **"is not in leaving the world, but in staying long enough to say the words you were afraid to speak."**

CHAPTER 8

THE STEPFAMILY'S GHOSTS

"The dead do not leave us; they linger in the sentences we never finished."- *Santiago Dagon*

The Stepsister's Absence

I learned about Sarah's death from a text. Call me when you can. It's about Sarah.

Morning light was barely in the room. I called at once. My mother's voice was flat in that careful way that tries to keep feelings from breaking open. "There was an accident," she said. I waited for the part that fixes things. "She's gone."

Sarah was twenty-four. She was my stepfather's daughter. For a few years she had lived with us, the two of us sharing a hallway and a sense that the adults were always busy loving someone else. She once kidded we were half related by trauma, then laughed like it was a good joke to keep nearby in case of emergency.

After the call I sat still and watched the wall. Then I did what I had taught myself to do when feeling arrived without permission. I opened the laptop. News. Emails. Music with no words. Nothing filled the room that the word gone had emptied.

"Grief arrives like a visitor we never invite but must still feed," Santiago wrote.

We had not seen each other in months. Mom's third divorce scattered everyone. I told myself I would reach out in time. Time is a promise that keeps changing its mind.

The funeral was small. Closed casket. Lilies and rain in the air. My mother clung to the arm of a new boyfriend with a face I could not place. Her mascara made small rivers that did not ask for directions.

My father came and stood at the back like a man attending history. He did not know Sarah well. He knew me. When our eyes met, he gave a nod that said more than we had managed with whole paragraphs. I am here.

After the service we stood outside and accepted quiet sentences from people who did not know where to place their hands. "She was such a good girl," Mom said, pressing her cheek against my coat. "She just got lost." No one asked if it was an accident. No one said the other word. I did not ask. Loss does not change its shape when we rename it.

I kept seeing her in small moments. A cigarette behind the garage. The tilted smile she wore when the room grew tense. The way she studied the sky as if it were sounding out her name. She had once told me she felt like a ghost in her own family. I shrugged it off because I did not know what to do with a sentence like that. Now I could hear it walking the house.

Grief Without Closure

Grief slows sound. The world continues, but the timing changes.

After the funeral, my father offered to drive me home. We listened to the wipers keep time on the windshield. When he parked, he rested his hands on the wheel and said, "I did not know her, but she seemed kind." "She was," I said. "I am sorry, son."

He had said those words before. This time they arrived softer. He looked past me for a moment, then spoke like a man thinking aloud. "It is strange. You try to raise children. You do your best. Then one day they are gone, and you understand how little you ever knew them."

I wanted to tell him thank you for coming. I wanted to say that his presence placed a hand on my shoulder the entire day. Instead, I said, "Yeah." The small word we use when large ones are afraid of heights.

"Death has a way of reopening the rooms we thought were closed," Santiago wrote.

For weeks I could not stop seeing the pieces of Sarah that never assembled for the adults in her life. The awkward laugh that arrived too early. The ashtray on the back step. The text she sent me once that I never answered. Miss you, J. I had meant to reply. Meaning to is the cousin of forgetting.

My father called a few days later. "How is your mother holding up?" "Not good." "And you?" "I am fine." Silence. Then he said, "Sometimes grief hits the living harder than the dead." "Why?" I asked. "It reminds us of who else we have lost."

He did not have to say the names. I felt them.

That night I cried. Not only for Sarah. For the unread messages, for the Sundays that passed without a call, for the versions of myself that kept waiting on the other side of a door I would not open. Grief is a mirror you look into hoping to see the one who is no longer there. Instead, it shows you the parts of yourself you abandoned while you were busy surviving.

How Death Redefines Family

People call more after a funeral. My mother and I talked in circles that could not decide where to land. She stepped between sadness and memory and blame as if the floor were uneven. One night she said, "I tried to be a good mother." Her voice did not ask for judgment, only rest. I did not answer. Some sentences are chairs for the soul; you offer them to another, and in their silence, they find a place to rest.

My father called again to check in. He never used the word grief. He asked about the car and the bills and whether the heater made that noise again. I used to treat those questions like a fence between us. Now I heard the care woven through them. Sarah's absence had shifted the furniture inside all of us.

When I visited, he made coffee that tasted like work. We sat at the table and listened to the house be a house. He spoke without preface. "I think about her," he said. "Me too." "She reminded me of you." "How?" "She carried too much alone."

He stared into his cup as if it were still making up its mind. "I should have said something to her," he added.

I began to repeat the usual comforts. You could not have known. You did what you could. But there is a kind of guilt that does not want relief. It only wants a witness. So I kept quiet and let the moment breathe.

"Sometimes death teaches us how to speak again," Santiago wrote. **"Not with words, but with presence."**

When I left, he hugged me and his hands trembled. "Take care of yourself, son." "You too, Dad."

We did not say I love you. Still, the room heard it. Love speaks through pauses when it cannot find the right words.

Sarah's death did not make anything neat. It did not stitch the past or absolve the living. What it did was remove the myth that time is generous. We began to meet more often. Not every week. Enough that the porch light felt like it was waiting for me specifically. We did not talk much about the past. We sat in the yard and watched the day do its quiet work. He watered the tomatoes as if they needed him personally. I watched the oak and tried to imagine the version of us that once sat beneath it.

Family is not only the people who share your last name. Family are the ones who keep showing up when showing up no longer promises reward. The ones who will stand near you while you hold the weight of a sentence that has no end.

Loss did not end our connection. It changed the path it took to reach us. It moved through small acts, through coffee poured too strong, through the hush of a car that stays in the driveway two minutes longer before pulling away.

"Loss does not end a relationship," Santiago Dagon wrote. **"It only changes the way love travels between the living and the gone."**

Sarah remains with me in unfinished ways. In the text that says *Miss you* and does not receive an answer. In the cigarette smoke rising like a signal no one learned to read. In my father's hands when they shake and still refuse to let go.

Grief has made our house different. Not louder. More honest. The rooms that once stored silence now hold presence. We do not have the right words. We have chairs and time and an agreement that being here counts. And on good days, it is enough.

CHAPTER 9

WHEN GRANDMOTHERS FADE

"The ones who held us the gentlest are the hardest to let go."- *Santiago Dagon*

The Matriarch's Hands

The last time I saw my grandmother, the afternoon light lay across her lap like a soft blessing. She was in her recliner by the window, the same spot where she had read, prayed, and waited for phone calls that rarely came. Her hands rested on a folded blanket she had crocheted years ago. They were thin and shaking now, a landscape of veins and memory.

She looked up and smiled, that small half-smile that seemed to carry forgiveness for everything you did not say. "You came," she whispered, her voice no louder than the ticking clock. "I told you I would." "I know," she said, eyes bright with both humor and knowing. "But words are easy. Showing up, that's the hard part."

It hit me deeper than I expected. I had said I'll visit soon so many times that the phrase had lost meaning. She had heard it before, from me, from my father, and from everyone who believed time would wait. But time does not wait. It steals softly, asking permission only after it is gone.

She reached for my hand. Her touch was warm and trembling, like something trying to stay. "You've grown quiet," she said. "I get that from the family," I told her, half smiling. She laughed. "No," she said, "You get quiet from pain."

I did not answer. She had always been able to see straight through me; past excuses, past the performances we put on for everyone else. When I was a boy, she had been my calm place, the one person who never picked sides after the divorce. She never tried to fix me. She just sat close enough to remind me I was not alone.

She told stories that day, not the grand kind, but the quiet ones. About sugar rations during the war, about the night she met my grandfather at a church dance, about the neighbors who once gathered for coffee on Sunday afternoons. "He was quiet," she said of my grandfather, smiling softly. "The good kind of quiet. Like your father."

For the first time, I heard the lineage differently. Maybe the silence passed down through our family was not failure. Maybe it was simply the way love survived when words ran out.

We talked for hours about ordinary things, the taste of peaches, the price of bread, and the kindness of strangers. When I finally stood to leave, she held my hand again and said, "Don't forget to remember."

I laughed then. It sounded like one of her riddles. It does not anymore.

"The dying speak in riddles that only time can translate," Santiago wrote.

Generational Grief

The call came on a Tuesday morning. My mother's voice was steady, as if it had rehearsed. "She passed last night. In her sleep."

I sat still, holding the phone to my ear. Silence filled the space where air should have been.

Grief does not always crash in. Sometimes it tiptoes, sits down beside you, and waits for you to notice.

I drove to her house the next day. The curtains were closed, but light still tried to find its way in. The smell of lavender hung in the air, mixed with something older, time itself.

Everything was exactly as she had left it: her reading glasses on the table, her teacup half full, her crossword puzzle unfinished. The last word she had filled in was grace.

I ran my fingers across the page. Somehow it felt deliberate, as if she had known those would be her final letters.

Mom was there, sorting papers with the distracted focus of someone trying not to collapse. "She didn't suffer," she said. I nodded, though suffering does not end with dying. It only changes addresses.

I walked from room to room touching her blankets, her books, her apron. The air carried her in everything. On her nightstand lay her Bible. Inside the front cover, in shaky handwriting, she had written: When you read this, remember that love is what remains.

That undid me. Tears came before I could stop them, not just for her, but for all the unfinished sentences in our family. For my father, who had not seen her in years. For Sarah. For the child version of me who thought love would always wait.

"Grief does not fade," Santiago wrote. **"It becomes a language of its own, a way of remembering that we were once loved deeply enough to ache."**

That night I called Dad. He answered on the second ring. "It's Grandma," I said. He didn't speak for a while. Then, quietly, "She was the best of us."

Neither of us could say more. But somewhere in the silence between our breathing, I heard something I had not heard in years, my father crying.

The Last Thread of Belonging

After the funeral, her house was emptied piece by piece. The photographs went to Mom, the linens to charity, the furniture to strangers who did not know how sacred the scratches were. I took her clock, the one that never kept proper time.

Each slow tick felt like she was still talking, saying, You're late, but you came anyway.

Dad could not travel for the service. His health had worsened, but he sent white lilies with a card that said only: For her kindness. That evening he called. "She was a good woman," he said. "She loved you," I told him. He was quiet for a long time. Then, "I know. I just wish I had said it back."

Something changed then, the tone gently softened. We talked longer than usual, about her biscuits, her stubborn faith, her endless patience. At one point he said, "She used to tell me that forgiveness keeps families alive." He paused, as if hearing his own words for the first time. "I think I understand what she meant now."

It was the closest he had ever come to, I am sorry. I didn't press it. Some apologies arrive as wind, you feel them, not hear them.

"When the elders fade," Santiago wrote, **"the map of belonging begins to blur. We must redraw it ourselves."**

That night I dreamed of her house. The bread smell lingered. The clock ticked. She sat by the window in her chair, smiling at me as if no time had passed at all. I reached for her hand. She said, "Tell your father it's not too late." Then she dissolved into light.

When I woke, the echo of her voice stayed in my chest like a heartbeat. It's not too late. Maybe she meant for him. Maybe for me.

I called him that morning. He sounded startled. "Everything okay?" "Yeah," I said. "Just wanted to talk. "He laughed softly. "About what?" "Nothing," I said. "Just talk."

We did. For nearly an hour. Weather, memories, how quiet the nights were now. He told me something I had never known that one Christmas, when money was tight, she had given him cash to buy me a present. She said, "Don't let pride get in the way of love."

When we hung up, I listened to the ticking of her clock. It still didn't keep time, but it kept something better. It kept rhythm.

Maybe that was her last lesson that love is not about being on time, but about still arriving.

"The heart learns rhythm from loss," Santiago Dagon wrote. **"Each goodbye teaches us how to love what remains."**

I sat there for a long while, watching the hands circle the face, steady and imperfect, keeping the kind of time that never ends.

PART III

--- ❧ ---

THE MIRROR OF TIME

CHAPTER 10

THE MAN IN THE MIRROR

"Forgiveness is not a doorway we walk through together. It is the courage to open it alone."- *Santiago Dagon*

Recognition

The year I felt my own strength as a man; my father recognized his advancing age. Two men at either end of the same bridge, both listening for footsteps that had not crossed in a while.

We had not spoken for months when his birthday came. I almost let the day pass. The old habit of delay felt familiar. Then my grandmother's voice rose in me like a bell. It is not too late. I dialed.

"Hello." "Hey, Dad. Happy birthday." A small pause. "Justin… thank you, son."

His voice was softer than I remembered. Slower. It carried calm inside it. We spoke about the yard, about a neighbor's fence, about the dog who had learned to sleep in sunbeams. I said I should come by soon. He said there was no rush, and I knew there was.

Before we hung up, he said, "You do not sound happy." "I learned that from you," I said. He did not defend himself. He sighed. "Maybe that is not something I should have passed on."

Something shifted again. I heard the first creak of a door we had both avoided. Age had peeled a layer from his voice. Less armor. More human. The kind of human I recognized.

That night I stood in front of the bathroom mirror. Thirty-five. The eyes looked like mine and like his. The brow carried our shared feature. The mouth felt tired from sentences that never reached the heart.

A truth rose that I could not step away from. I had become the thing I resisted. A man afraid of his own softness.

"We grow into our fathers whether we mean to or not," Santiago wrote. **"The heart remembers its teachers, even when it swears it will not."**

The next week I drove over without a reason. I told myself it was a quick visit. Instinct knew better. He opened the door. He looked smaller, as if time had loosened him at the edges. But the smile was familiar. The same one from the county fair when his shoulders were still a throne.

"Did not think I would see you," he said. "I needed to come."

We sat in the living room with the old coffee. He poured two cups and admitted he could not drink it black anymore. I said we were both getting old. He said we were getting honest.

We talked for hours about the present, not the past. My work. His naps. The way the oak looked different in afternoon light. It felt ordinary. Ordinary turned out to be what healing had been asking for all along.

When I stood to leave, he hugged me a moment longer than before. "I am glad you came, son." "I am too," I said, and for the first time in years I meant it without needing to run.

Later I faced the mirror again. The same face. The same shared longing to make peace. I did not see only myself. I saw him in me, and me in him, like two reflections on the same water.

Inherited Regret

Regret is not a memory. It is a current. It moves through a family the way a river moves through a valley, shaping everything it passes.

For years I believed my father had chosen distance. Now I could name its source. It had been handed to him in silence the way a pocket watch is handed down to a son. He once told me his father never said I love you. Not once. "He showed it," Dad said. "How?" I asked. "He worked. He stayed. He fixed what broke." "Did it feel like love?" "It did then," he said. "You miss the words when you get older."

I recognized my own pattern in his answer. He built walls from silence. I built mine from motion and screens. Different materials. Same design.

"We inherit more than names," Santiago wrote. "We inherit the unfinished apologies our parents never found the breath to speak."

A few months after that visit his body slowed. More medicine bottles. Longer sleeps. Steps that paused halfway through rooms as if the next step needed permission. He brushed it off. He liked to say aging was only a schedule change. But his eyes began to hold me longer, as if he were memorizing what he might forget.

We sat beneath the oak he planted the year I was born. The shade moved across our shoes like a slow tide. "You ever think about how fast it all goes," he said. "All the time." "I thought I would have more time to get it right." "With what?" He smiled without teeth. "Being your dad."

I wanted to say he had done more right than he believed. The sentences lined up and waited for me to be brave. They stayed on the tongue like guests who would not step through the doorway. He wanted forgiveness but did not know how to ask. I wanted connection but did not know how to offer. So, we sat together and let the tree speak for us.

My grandmother's last words returned. Do not forget to remember. Perhaps that was her way of saying that remembering is a form of forgiveness. You let the whole story walk in, not only the parts that fit a grievance.

He fell asleep in his chair that evening, mouth open the way children sleep when the day has taken every last bit of them. I watched his chest rise and fall and said the words I could not wake him to hear. I love you. I do not blame you. You did enough.

They were quiet sentences. They felt like a key turning in a lock that had been painted shut.

The Beginning of Self-Forgiveness

Change did not announce itself. It arrived as small permissions. I started to see what he had given. He stayed. He worked. He showed up the best way he could. I began to tell the truth about myself too. I had not been easy to reach. I had kept my door closed and then criticized him for not knocking harder.

We speak of forgiveness as a gift we offer to another. It is also a mercy we owe our own heart for carrying too much for too long.

"Forgiveness is how love remembers itself," Santiago wrote.

I started to see my father as a man before I saw him as a father. A boy raised by a silent veteran. A teenager praised for endurance and not for softness. A young man who learned to hold tears until they salted him from the inside. A middle-aged father who believed firmness was the same as safety. An old man who finally knew the cost.

I visited more. We kept our language simple. We raked the leaves. We patched fence. We checked batteries in flashlights. We replaced the porch light even when it had not burned out. Presence began to do the work we had asked words to do alone.

One evening as we lined up new pickets for the fence Jack said, "My father made me do this when I was a kid." "You hated it," I joked. "I did," he chuckled. "Because it felt like punishment. Now I think it was a way to keep me close without admitting he needed me."

He looked at me. "I suppose I did the same thing with you." I nodded. The truth did not sting. It satisfied. Like a lost piece of a puzzle finally clicking into place.

When we finished, he stood back to admire what we had built. The fence was not straight. Neither were we. It stood anyway.

As I was leaving, he said, "You turned out good, son. Better than I did." "No," I answered. "You just turned out first." He laughed and shook his head. "That is one way to put it."

A week later his heart stumbled. The doctor called it a warning. I called it the sound of the clock reminding us we could not afford the old delays. He phoned from the hospital with a voice that had traveled a long way in a short time. "Do not worry," he said. "I am not done yet." "Neither am I," I told him, and for once I knew exactly what I meant.

That night I returned to the mirror. The face was ours again. But the look had changed. It was less guarded. It carried light the way windows do at dusk. I understood something I had not allowed before. Healing does not require a new story. It requires the courage to love the one we lived.

Forgiveness gathered in me like water after a slow thaw. At first it sounded like acceptance. Then it began to sound like freedom. I could breathe without the weight of old sentences pressing on my lungs.

I stood there a long while and practiced saying what I had been saving for the right moment. "I forgive you, Dad," I whispered. I let the words stand on the tile and listen to themselves. Then I added the one that finished the work. "I forgive me too."

"Every son must meet his father twice," Santiago Dagon wrote. **"Once in childhood when he is still a hero. And again, in adulthood when he becomes human. Only then can love begin."**

The mirror did not change. I did. I walked out of the room with a quieter heart and a steadier step, ready to build a bridge that did not need to be perfect to hold. The door I had feared for years had been open the whole time. I finally had the courage to walk through it alone, so I could meet my father on the other side.

CHAPTER 11

THE SON WHO CAME HOME

"Sometimes we come home not to find the people we love, but to remember the parts of ourselves we left behind."   - *Santiago Dagon*

The Awkward Reunion

The late spring morning wrapped the road in a soft haze. The porch light was on though the sun was up for several hours. He always did that. A light that waited, even in daylight.

When I called to ask if I could stay a while, he did not hesitate. "Of course," he said. His voice caught, then cleared. "You do not have to ask."

He stood in the doorway as I pulled in. Thinner. Smaller in the frame. The smile made him taller. "Hey, son." "Hey, Dad."

The hug was brief. A careful agreement. We each measured how much weight the other could hold. Inside, the rooms still kept the same arrangement. The chair by the window. The coffee ring on the table. The faint scent of the aging house had grown edged with musk. Familiarity settled on my shoulders and pressed down. Memory is heavier than it looks.

"I cleared the guest room," he said. "Fresh sheets. Thanks."

We spent that first evening on easy ground. Weather. Groceries. A neighbor's dog that barked at passing clouds. He did not ask why I had really returned. I did not volunteer it. Grown men often prefer an honest task to an honest sentence.

That night I lay in the bed where a boy once planned his escape. The old house breathed around me. A stair answered its own creak. A pipe sighed in the wall. I heard his steps and knew where he paused, where he turned off the lamp, where he stood an extra beat as if remembering something gentle.

Morning arrived with the sound of a kettle. He poured two cups and slid one toward me with the shy pride of a host. "Got some work if you are up for it." "I am."

It was not much. A small bridge built from routine. But it held.

Work as Language

He did not speak love with long words. He spoke it with a tool in his hand. Fixing was his grammar. Repair was his tense.

We started with the fence along the back field. Years of weather had pulled it out of true. He handed me a hammer. "Do not hit your thumb this time," he said, grinning at a memory that was more tender than it sounded.

I laughed, then felt the old spark of defense. "You always think I cannot do things." He looked up, surprised. "That is not what I meant." "I know," I said too quickly.

The air paused. Then we worked. The rhythm did what words could not. Pull. Set. Strike. Slower for him now. Careful steps. Careful breaths. The hands still knew what to do.

"You do not need to do all of it," I said when he leaned on the post to rest. "If I stop moving, I will stop," he answered, smiling without apology.

We straightened a line of boards that had been leaning for years. He stepped back and admired what stood. "Looks right," he said. "We are a good team," I answered. He nodded, almost embarrassed by the agreement.

On the porch he poured tea over ice and watched the yard think about evening. He kept looking over at me as if checking a map. "What," I asked, finally. "Nothing," he said. "Just proud." "Thanks."

It should have been enough. But an old ache stirred. "You do not have to try so hard," I said. He tilted his head. "Try at what?" "At making things better." He looked out over the field. "I have been trying my whole life. I do not know how to stop."

The next morning, he asked if I would help with the shed. I sighed before I could stop myself. "I guess."

He heard the weight in it. "You guess." "I thought we might talk more," I said. "Not only fix things." He set the wrench down. "Talking is not easy for me, Justin. You know that." "That is part of the problem," I said, softer than it felt.

The words hung there. We let them. We spent the afternoon quietly working. Nails and hammer, the sound of two people who needed more than they could say.

That night he watched an old western. A hero who rode into town and solved things by standing still. I watched him watch it. I finally understood that every project, every chore, every cup left beside my hand was his way of saying what he could not form in speech. I wanted the words. He offered the work. Both were love. I was not ready to accept that both could be true.

The Unspoken Goodbye

The weeks took on a careful shape. We shared a roof and a schedule. We spoke in the safe rooms. Small talk. Small tasks. Long silences that were beginning to feel less like walls and more like rooms we both knew how to enter.

Old habits rose like weeds. I rolled my eyes at his cautions. I mocked his slower pace under my breath, then hated myself for it. It was not cruelty. It was fear in a coat I had worn for years.

One evening he stood at the window and studied the oak. "Something wrong," I asked. "Just thinking," he said. "That tree has been here as long as you." "Yeah." "We have both taken our share of weather. "His tone was different. Not stern. Not resigned. A soft acceptance that sounded like a man making peace with the math of his days.

"You will understand someday," he said. "I am trying." "I know."

A few days later he fell in the garden. Only a stumble. Only a bruise. But seeing him there on the ground unclipped something in me. "Slow down," I said as I helped him inside. "If I slow down, I will stop breathing," he joked. "You are not invincible." "Never said I was," he answered, and then, after a breath, "But I am not done yet."

We sat with that. The room felt fragile, like glass cupped between warm hands.

He looked at the floor and spoke without raising his head. "I know I was not easy to love." "Dad-" "Let me say this."

His voice trembled, and I realized he had rehearsed these lines in empty rooms. "I made mistakes. I thought working hard would fix them. I thought doing the right thing was the same as saying the right thing. It was not." He swallowed. "You deserved better. I hope you know I tried."

His eyes were wet. I had never seen him cry. The sight of it closed my throat. I wanted to say the words that would lift his shoulder out from under all that weight. I could not find them. So I nodded. "I know," I said, and meant it with my whole chest.

That night I heard him coughing. I stood in the hallway and listened until it stopped. I almost knocked. I did not. I told myself I would check on him in the morning. The heart is not a calendar.

At dawn I walked the back road to clear my head. When I returned, his coffee was cooling on the table. He was in the recliner, turned slightly toward the window, eyes fixed on a place where the light gathered. "You okay," I asked. "Just tired," he said. "Just tired, son."

I did not know those would be the last true words. I left home with him in the care of a hospice nurse.

A few days later, the house stirred with red lights. They swept across yard onto the porch. The paramedics arrived, kind and skilled. By then, it was already over.

I rushed over, stood on the steps with my hands empty, my pain too loud for tears. Inside, his mug waited with a small ring of heat left in it. His phone buzzed once with a message from me that would never be read. The porch light was on.

"We do not always get to say goodbye," Santiago wrote. **"Sometimes the goodbye is in the things left waiting for us. A cup. A porch light. A name we still whisper in an empty house."**

I walked the rooms and touched what he had touched. A pencil on the table. A list in his handwriting. A note in his wallet that I had not yet found. Breathing felt like carrying something heavy up a narrow stair.

Between grief and guilt a quiet truth rose. I had not come home to fix him. I had come home to understand him. The fixing had been his language. The understanding had to be mine.

On the porch the evening came with long shadows across the yard. The fence we straightened stood firm in its new line. The oak kept watch. For the first time I could see what he had built with all that quiet. Not only a house. A record of trying. Not perfect. Steady.

"In every house there is a silence that remembers the voice that filled it," Santiago Dagon wrote. **"Listen long enough, and you will hear that love never left. It simply changed its sound."**

I stood beneath the porch light and let it hold me. I said his name into the dusk. It did not answer. But something in me did. I was still his son. He was still my father. The work remained. So did the love.

CHAPTER 12

THE VISIT HOME

"The dead do not vanish, they change their address, from the body to the memory."- *Santiago Dagon*

Time's Soft Warnings

It took almost three years to turn the car into the gravel drive. I told myself I was here to settle things, to clear rooms, to make decisions. That was the story I could carry. The truer reason sat lower in the chest. The silence between us had outlived him. I did not want it to outlive me.

The fence we had set back in line was still holding, though two boards leaned as if they missed his hands. The oak had spread its shade across half the yard, a quiet cathedral that asked for nothing. The porch light worked. He always chose bulbs that lasted longer than anyone expected. They shone in daylight too, a small act of faith and hope.

I stayed in the car and watched the door. It used to open before I could knock. Now it waited like a sealed envelope. When I stepped inside the smell met me. Old wood, the whisper of coffee that never leaves a house that has been lived in and loved.

His chair kept its place by the window. The clock ticked as if it had been counting for both of us. The rooms did not feel empty. They felt full of what had been said, and of what had not.

I stood at the counter; my palm rested on the worn spot where his mug used to occupy. The cup hung on the rack with its chipped handle and the stain that never washed out. I took it down and turned it in my hand.

"Hey, Dad," I said, and the sound of my own voice surprised me.

"The living speak to the dead not because they expect an answer," Santiago wrote, **"but because silence is too heavy to hold alone."**

I made coffee that tasted like his. Black. Bitter. I lifted it like a small ritual, not to feel better, only to feel him.

The wind moved through the oak and the house breathed. I could almost hear his steps, the soft clear of his throat, the way he stood a moment before he spoke. Coming back hurt. Love and pain, it turns out, kept the same forwarding address.

The Father's Decline

After the funeral I told careful sentences that help others stand near you. He lived a good life. He went peacefully. He is in a better place. The ache did not listen.

Grief does not leave. It learns new shapes. At first it is sharp, then it becomes dull and patient. It waits in the sound of one cup set gently on a table. It waits in the sight of a jacket that still holds a shoulder.

His decline began the way winter begins, in small air, with nothing that looks like snow. "Only tired," he said. "Getting older," he said. I watched his hands when he lifted the compost bag to feed the garden and saw how effort took his breath for a second longer than it used to.

I would say "Let me." "I have been doing this my whole life," he answered. "Not at thirty," I said. He laughed and said some days still felt like thirty. We both knew that was a story kindness tells.

During his last days he called less. Not for lack of wanting, but because a call asks for breath. His texts shortened. Doing okay? You good. I answered with one word and the day moved on. A full conversation between a tired father and a distracted son, finished before the heart arrived.

Death comes with small signs like coins in a dish. Mail left unopened. Coffee cooled before half the cup was gone. The small tremor when he reached for the remote. He hid it the way he always did, inside a joke, behind a question about my work.

I remembered him holding the photo from the county fair, the one where I am on his shoulders and the sun thrones us both. "You remember that day," I asked. "Of course," he said. "You dropped ice cream on my hair." "You yelled at me." He shook his head. "I yelled because I was scared you would cry. I did not want you to see me lose it."

That was his vocabulary. Tenderness hid behind irritation. Love wore the uniform of duty.

A notebook sat by his chair near the end. He said it was for doctor notes. After he died, I opened it. Short lines covered the pages, half list, half confession. One sentence stopped me. I do not know how to say it right, but I loved him every day.

I closed the book and held it the way you hold something that has heat of its own. Love does not always arrive in the form we want. Sometimes it arrives as labor. Sometimes it arrives as a man who shows up repeatedly without the right words. Or the house door always open with welcome. And somehow that is the hidden word Love.

I told others he went peacefully in sleep. Peacefully is a clean word. Life is not clean. Neither is love.

Grief does not hand out closure. It offers recognition. I began to understand. Death does not carry the love away. It leaves it on the table and waits for you to notice.

The Last Shared Light

I stayed three days because leaving felt like a second funeral. The house asked nothing from me except attention. Each room had a sentence that needed a listener.

That first night, I sat beside the lamp near his chair. I turned it on and let its quiet hum breathe beside me. Its shade cast a soft gold across the room, the same light that once fell over his hands while old westerns played.

On the second day I cleaned to escape my sorrow. I washed his mug. I folded shirts that still knew his shoulders. I made neat stacks of books he would have reorganized the moment I left the room. In the bedside drawer I found the small things he could never throw away. A drawing I made in second grade. A photograph of him and my mother when the air still held their future. A tube of wood glue that had already dried at the cap. A square of paper in his unsteady hand that said, Do not forget to water the oak.

Toward evening I went out to the yard. The light folded through the leaves like blessings that did not need a name. I put my hand on the bark and felt the rough truth of time. "I am here," I said. "I am still here."

A wind moved through and made a sound that trees make when they choose to answer. I called it a yes.

"When the living speak softly enough, the dead can still hear them," Santiago wrote.

I stayed until stars showed their first quiet fires. He had once pointed to them and said, "We will all be stars someday, just different kinds." I used to think he meant heaven. Now I think he meant continuation. Not an ending, a change of form.

On the third morning I stood in the doorway and looked back. The house seemed smaller in the bright sunlight. The porch light was still on. I did not turn it off. It felt wrong to end a sentence that was still speaking.

Love is not a rescue from the dark. It is a light that says you are not alone. I closed the door and stepped into the day with that light inside my heart. The silence between us did not feel empty anymore. It felt full, full of everything we never said and everything we meant.

"The end of a story is not where love dies," Santiago Dagon wrote. **"It is where love learns to live without being seen."**

I drove away slowly, then a little faster, then at the pace the road allowed. In the mirror I watched the porch light grow small and then smaller until the curve took it from view. It was still there. It would be there tonight. It would be there in memory when the bulb finally failed. And I would be here, watering the oak, learning the steady work of carrying what remains.

PART IV

❧

THE QUIET UNDERSTANDING

CHAPTER 13

THE CONVERSATION WE WAITED
A LIFETIME FOR

"Death does not silence love, it simply changes who does the listening."- *Santiago Dagon*

Breaking the Wall

I came back to the oak on an afternoon that felt like time was suspended between moments. No flowers. No folded note. No ceremony. Just me, and the tree we planted with hope we did not know how to name.

The grass at the base had gone long and soft. The wind passed through the leaves with the patience of an old friend. I could almost see him there, the worn jacket, the mug, the half-smile that meant he cared more than he could say.

"I am not here to cry," I said. "I am here to speak."

For years, the conversation lived inside me, heavy and unfinished. Unread messages. Unsent apologies. The pain of a door that was always almost open.

When someone dies their voice does not leave. It moves inward. It talks in your thoughts. It waits in your pauses. It rises in your choices.

"Hey, Dad," I said, and my voice broke on the second word. I waited for a sign. There was no sign. Only air, only leaves, only time that refused to hurry.

"So," I said, "here is the truth. I do not know where to begin. There is too much of it, and none of it feels enough." I laughed once, quiet and honest. "That is how you started your sentences too. Half finished. Hoping the rest would arrive on its own."

A tear found its way, and I let it go where it wanted. "I miss you." Simple. Late. True.

I leaned back against the trunk and let the bark press its memory into my shoulder. "I thought your dying would make this easier," I said. "That grief would fade. That time would sand down all the sharp places. It did not. It is not time that heals. It is truth. I never gave you mine."

The wind moved like a careful breath. "Here is what I know now," I said. "I blamed you for years. For the silence. For the distance. For not knowing how to give the words I needed. I said you did not care. I said you did not understand. I did not understand either. You were doing the best you could with the tools you were handed. No one gave you the language for tenderness. No one asked you to name your pain. And I did to others what I accused you of doing to me. I hid. I judged. I mistook strength for silence."

I pressed my palm to the ground as if it could hold the weight I was setting down.

"The hardest apologies," Santiago wrote, **"are the ones that must cross the distance between worlds."**

Above me the clouds thinned. Light found a path through the leaves and rested on my hands. I did not call it a sign. I called it welcome.

This was the right place to lay the words. The tree had been listening since we set it into the earth. It knew our arguments. It knew our trying. It knew the love that worked with tools and could not find its voice.

Words Finally Spoken

"Do you remember the times I called you stupid," I asked the air. "Of course you do. I said it more than once. "I said it because I was afraid. Mocking felt like strength. It was not. You were never stupid. You were patient. You were stubborn in a way that was really faith. You kept going. You did not quit. I never thanked you for that."

I swallowed. The old habit tried to close my throat. I opened it with care. "You always asked if I needed anything. I always said no. I should have said yes. I needed you. Not your money. Not a lecture. Just you. I needed to know I mattered to you in the way you already knew you mattered to me."

A small bird landed on a low branch and tilted its head as if attending. "Even the birds are tired of my silence," I said, and I smiled for the first time.

"After you died, I waited for wisdom to arrive," I went on. "I wanted grief to turn into clean meaning. Mostly it turned into anger. I was angry at myself for waiting. Angry at you for leaving before I learned to speak. Angry at time for being time."

I looked up through the green. "Maybe love is always late," I said. "Maybe memory is how we finish the conversations that life could not hold."

The next words were small and clear. "I forgive you." I let them sit in the shade where we could both see them.

"For the yelling," I added. "For the days you chose work instead of talk. For the times you tried to protect me with distance." I forgive the man who was learning as he went. I breathed in and did not rush the next sentence. "And I am asking for your forgiveness too. For my pride. For my vanishing. For judging you by a standard I did not meet myself. You loved in actions. I wanted the comfort of words. We were both right, and we were both wrong."

I closed my eyes. "I love you." Said out loud at last. Said like a key in a lock.

The light shifted. Warmth found my neck. "You always said the weather knew when to behave," I whispered.

I sat and let the good ache spread. All my life I had waited for you to say I was enough. I can see now that you did. You said it in car drives at dawn. You said it in fences made straight. You said it in the porch light that waited for me even in daylight. Presence is a sentence. I am finally fluent.

I put my hand on the trunk and felt the slow pulse of the living wood. "I hear you now," I said.

The Quiet Peace

Dusk began its soft work while I stood to leave. Shadows laid themselves down across the yard like blankets. The air cooled and the world entered that tender space between day and night where everything grows gentle enough to listen.

The house did not look like a museum anymore. It looked like a memory that had learned to breathe. I walked from room to room, and nothing reached to hurt me. The chair was a chair. The lamp was a lamp. Grief had loosened its grip and handed the rooms back to themselves.

I turned on the small lamp by his recliner. The shade poured its warm circle across the table the same way it once fell across his hands. "You always said lamps make a house less lonely," I said. "You were right."

I sat where he sat and let the cushion give. A simple peace arrived. Not the kind that erases pain. The kind that makes space for the love beneath it.

I understood forgiveness as something different now. It is not a pardon for the past. It is permission for the heart to travel light. It is the way we tell one another you do not owe me anymore. It is the way we tell ourselves, neither do you.

"I think I am going to be okay," I said to the empty room that was not empty.

"Peace does not arrive when the pain disappears," Santiago wrote. **"It arrives when the love underneath the pain finally has room to breathe."**

I stood, and I turned off the lamp. The last light faded at a kind pace. I stepped onto the porch and touched the rail we sanded together. Then I went to the oak once more, not to speak, only to place my palm where the bark meets air. "Thank you," I said. "For the work. For the tries. For being my father while I learned how to be your son."

The wind moved through with the scent of earth and the hint of rain. I did not feel alone. I felt accompanied by an echo that did not need sound to be true.

The porch light above the door came on by itself. I smiled the way you smile at a familiar joke.

"Okay, Dad," I said. "I see you."

Some conversations never end. They become the soft lamp in the house, and the steady light over the door, and the living tree that keeps our names.

CHAPTER 14

WHAT REMAINS OF LOVE

"Grief does not empty the heart, it teaches it to hold more than it thought it could."- *Santiago Dagon*

The Empty Chair

I returned over the years, the house stood still keeping a quiet that was not peace, only a long breath the walls refused to release. I sat in his chair, the one I teased him about for years. I used to tell him he would become the chair if he kept napping in it. He would lean back, lift his eyebrows, and say there were worse things to become. Now the cushion rose against my ribs with the same old give, and the empty curve where his shoulder once settled felt like a small shoreline where the tide no longer returned.

I could not move the chair. Some things are not furniture, they are evidence. The faint ring of his mug on the side table looked like a circle of belonging that had refused to fade. The jacket still hung by the door with its gentle sag. His boots waited with their quiet patience. The hallway held the soft scent of cedar that no window could carry away.

Grief did not come as a wave. It came as a list of small facts. A note folded once and left in a drawer. A pencil worn at the tip. A lid that still squeaked the way it did when he winced and promised he would fix it. The ordinary kept bending the light toward him. I had come to empty rooms and make order. What I really came for was proof that love does not vanish when the body steps away.

"The heart has its own geography," Santiago wrote, **"and we return to the coordinates where love first learned to ache."**

Every photograph asked to be touched. Every drawer felt like a request for permission. I kept saying I am sorry, to no one and to him. I am sorry I did not call. I am sorry I thought I knew the right way to love. I am sorry I waited for you to change instead of learning your language.

On his nightstand the notebook waited. I had read it before. I opened it again and turned to the last page, as if a different ending might have appeared while I was gone. The final line was as simple and undefended as a prayer.

Love does not die, it waits to be recognized.

I closed the book against my chest and stood by the window until the ache found a place to sit. Recognition came like a slow light. His love had always lived in labor. In mended things. In the porch light that stubbornly waited through daylight too. He had not spoken in the language I demanded. He spoke in the language he had been taught. He did not stop trying.

The Weight of Regret

Time did not heal anything. It only taught me the posture I needed to carry the weight without dropping everything else. At work I was fine. In rooms with friends, I was fine. Fine is a coat you wear when the weather inside you is not ready to be seen.

Regret did not shout. It preferred corners. It came when a radio station found one of his old songs. It came when a mirror offered back my face at an angle that held his eyes. It came when someone asked about my father and I did not know how to translate a love that did not live in sentences.

For years I was angry at him for what he did not say. Now I was angry at myself for what I did not hear. I borrowed opinions from voices that did not know him. They taught me to measure love by volume and display. I went looking for the love I had been promised on screens. I missed the love a man was building right in front of me with his hands.

His love looked like repaired fences. It looked like long drives he did not need to make. It looked like a wallet that opened farther than it should. It looked like the little food he saved and the better food he gave away. It looked like the light on the porch, waiting for footsteps that were late again.

I called it duty when I was young because I did not want to admit I needed it. Distance felt like independence. But distance only empties the cup. You still have to drink.

I replayed our worst days and our sharpest words until the scenes wore thin. Those fights felt like definition once. Now they felt like poor translations. Two people trying to reach each other through inherited vocabulary and running out of air.

He used to say you will understand someday. I rolled my eyes and put the sentence on the shelf where clichés go. Understanding arrived late, and with it came the kind of sorrow that time does not negotiate. I wanted to tell him I saw him at last, not as a standard he failed or as a mistake I carried, but as a man who fought his father's weather and still found a way to shelter me.

Forgiveness changed shape in those years. I thought it was a blessing we hand to others from a superior height. It turned out to be a necessity. You put the stone down because you cannot keep walking with it. You set it gently on the ground and honor where it took you, then you step forward with a chest that can breathe again.

"We do not heal by forgetting," Santiago wrote. **"We heal by remembering with tenderness."**

So I remembered tenderly. The half smile he saved for quiet victories. The way he looked at me when he believed I was not watching. The sound of his laugh when he was alone with the dog and thought no one could hear.

The Echo of Forgiveness

I told myself the closets were empty, and the drawers were clean. The house said, not yet. It did not feel like a tomb anymore. It felt like a witness who had decided to testify in my favor.

For years I thought love should be loud so I could not miss it. Now I understand that the quiet is what remains. Public love is beautiful. Humble love keeps the roof on.

He did not say I am proud of you enough. He said it every time he showed up. He did not say I love you with the ease I wanted. He said it with the thousand small gestures that stitched our days together.

I had chased a picture of love that never had dirt under its nails. Real love works. Real love repairs. Real love carries and does not count.

"You were right," I said. "About more than I wanted to admit."

"The dead forgive us long before we forgive ourselves," Santiago wrote. **"They do not keep score. They keep love."**

The oak continued to mature. I often stood beneath it and laid my palm on the bark the way you place a hand on a shoulder you trust. "I forgive you," I said. Words that linger toward the harder truth, "I forgive me."

It was not an ending. It was the echo that remains when the voice has taught you everything it can. It was love, still here, stripped of performance and pretense, patient as the earth, faithful as light over a door that remembers your name.

CHAPTER 15

LETTERS TO MY FATHER

"There are letters that learn our names, then wait inside the chest for the day we are brave."- *Santiago Dagon*

Words Never Sent

Dear Dad,

I have started this line a hundred times. Each time the pen lifts its head like a small animal and then curls back to sleep. I tell myself I will write the whole truth. I tell myself I will keep it simple. I tell myself I will not look away. Then the breath shortens and the page turns to glass.

You were the one who struggled with words. Now I am the one stumbling. Perhaps this is how inheritance works. Not only the jawline. Not only the hands. We receive what our parents could not say, and we spend the rest of our lives trying to teach it a language.

The first letter was brief. I wrote what I had carried for years.

I am sorry I chose to be right over being kind. I am sorry I mocked the weight you carried. I am sorry I did not see the boy inside the man who still needed a father.

I stopped there. The ink went dry while my heart kept running. I told myself a letter to the dead did not matter. I tore the page and lit it. Fire turned it into a memory I could control. The ash went soft. The ache stayed.

I wanted to tell you I understand now. The long days. The quiet nights. The slow walk to the porch where the light was both lantern and prayer. You were not cold. You were carrying too much. Silence was deep feelings that could not find words. Endurance was your proof. You did not leave. You did not stop. You loved with the tools you knew.

You once said I would understand someday. I do. It hurts.

Here is the part I never said aloud. I was proud of you. I was proud of the man who kept the lights on. I was proud of the hands that could fix what other men threw away. I thought pride was a river that only ran from father to son. I did not know a father waits to hear it back and grows older waiting.

You changed my tire during a storm and winced when you lifted the jack. I said thanks like you were a casual stranger at a store. I should have said you always show up for me. I should have said I see you. I should have said I am learning from your stubborn love. I did not. I was busy wanting poetry while you were building shelter.

Now I catch your reflection in the small things. The way I stand at the sink. The way I fold a bill twice before I put it away. The way I pause at a door and listen before I knock.

Death did not end our conversation. It changed the frequency. I hear you in the quiet between tasks. I hear you in the restraint that visits my tongue before I speak. I hear you in the old lesson I once refused. Keep going. Be decent. Mend what is within your reach.

Dad, I was proud of you. Dad, I am still learning how to say it.

"We inherit our parents' unfinished sentences and finish them in our own breath."- *Santiago Dagon*

Letters for the Living

If I could hand a note to any father, it would say this:

Tell your son what you see when you look at him. Not his grades. Not his paycheck. The good man in him. Say you are proud at ordinary times. Say it when he fails. Say it when he tries. Pride is not a medal. It is a lamp.

Ask him about his fear. Ask him about the place in his chest that goes quiet at night. He may not answer. Ask again next week. Ask again next year. Your repetition is a bridge.

If I could hand a note to any son, it would say this:

Your father's silence is not proof of absence. It is a habit he learned passed forward by a former generation. He may never say the sentence you want in the way you want to hear it. Listen to the way he holds the door. Listen to the way he pays first. Listen to the way he says drive safe and means come home.

Do not wait for a perfect moment. It does not exist. Use this afternoon. Use the drive between errands. Use the pause in the hallway. Tell him you see him. Tell him you are trying. Tell him you forgive what he did not know how to learn.

I will write one more note to the younger me.

Do not confuse distance with strength. Do not fashion pride into armor you cannot take off. Do not practice cleverness when tenderness is possible. Sit with the man who raised you and ask one question about the boy he was. Then listen until his eyes change. That is the doorway.

"To heal a family, speak one brave sentence before the day ends."- *Santiago Dagon*

Understanding Too Late

Love is not gentle by default. Love is a worker. It lifts. It repeats. It returns with another nail when the first one bends. I wanted love to be art. You showed me love is also carpentry.

I used to wish you were another man. A man who cried easily. A man who told long stories. A man who fit a picture in my head. If you had been that man, I might have missed the lesson only you could teach. Strength that does not boast. Fidelity that does not announce itself. A goodness that does not require applause.

I failed you in ways I now understand. I took your steadiness for granted. I mistook your restraint for judgment. I let other people's definitions of love become my measure. I withheld simple words that could have loosened your shoulders for a single evening. I cannot fix that. I can only refuse to pass it forward.

Sometimes I dream an ordinary dream. We are in the kitchen. The lamp is on. Your hands are clean for once. I say you did your best. You say so did you. We both nod like men who have finally found the same sentence. I wake with tear salt on my face and a soft ache that does not demand to be solved.

Grief is not the absence of love. Grief is love changing shape so it can stay. I see it now. In the way I wait an extra second before I speak. In the way I let another driver merge. In the way I fix something small and think of your hands. You are gone from the chair. You are not gone from the room.

"The dead remain where love keeps working."- *Santiago Dagon*

I do not force a perfect letter. I will write a true one.

Dad,

You did enough. You were enough. I am enough. I know this now.

I folded the page without sealing it. I place it in the drawer where you kept the spare batteries and the tape that always stuck to itself. I leave it there like a seed.

When I step outside our home, the evening is kind. The oak is speaking in leaf-syllables only the heart can hear. I looked up and said the line we both waited for. "Thank you for not quitting on me."

PART V

THE LIGHT THAT STAYS

FINAL EPILOGUE

THE HOUSE AT DUSK

"Love does not die with the body. It lingers, like light left behind on the walls after sunset."- *Santiago Dagon*

The house stands in its familiar hush. Not the silence of abandonment, but the kind that listens. The kind that remembers. Evening air moves through the screens, carrying the scent of rain and wood and the faint sweetness of cut grass. Each sound feels softer now: the slow tick of the old clock, the small shift of the rafters as the air cools, the sigh of wind against the windowpane.

Dust floats in the amber light. Each particle drifts like a slow prayer. The chair remains by the window, facing west. The lamp keeps its quiet watch, its shade golden even when unlit. The faint ring on the coffee table - from the cup that always sat beside him - has deepened into the wood. Some marks are meant to stay.

Outside, dusk folds itself into the yard. The sky moves from gold to honey, from honey to violet, then to the calm blue-gray of memory. The oak stands where it always has, its branches wide and unhurried. When the wind passes through, the leaves sound like whispers, not speech, but something close to recognition.

If you stand in the doorway long enough, you can almost feel them. The two of them. Father and son. Not as they were in their hardest years, but as they became: quiet, forgiven, understood. The old hurt no longer sharp, the distance finally bridged by time's soft hands.

There is something holy in forgiveness that arrives late. It cannot fix the past, but it can bless it. Santiago once wrote, **"The heart heals not by forgetting, but by remembering gently."** That is what this home is doing, remembering gently.

On the mantle, the photograph waits. The two of them at the oak, sunlight behind their shoulders. The father's hand rests lightly on his son's arm, not as ownership, but as a sign: I tried. The son's smile is uncertain, yet genuine as if that single moment taught him that love had always been there, only quiet, only waiting.

The image has faded with years, but the fading feels merciful. Memory learns to soften the edges, leaving behind only what is needed: the tenderness, the lesson, the light.

As the last birds call out, the day exhales. Shadows stretch across the floor. The lamp flickers once, then steadies, throwing its circle of gold upon the chair. It is enough.

If you listen closely, you can almost hear the father's voice, low and calm: "It is all right, son. I never really left."

And the son, older now, answers into the half-light: "I know."

Their words dissolve into the room, into the slow rhythm of evening settling over everything. The refrigerator hums its quiet reassurance. The floorboards creak in their familiar way. The air turns cool and kind.

Outside, the oak bends slightly with the breeze, its roots deep, its branches reaching toward the first stars. It stands as witness to the work of love, to the forgiveness that took a lifetime, to the small unbreakable bond between presence and memory.

The house at dusk holds them both one gone, one living in a peace that no longer needs words.

"In the end," Santiago Dagon wrote, **"the heart does not keep count of who left or who stayed. It remembers only who tried."**

And in that tender light between day and night, two hearts, one still beating, one long folded into the earth, move together in the same rhythm at last.

POSTSCRIPT

WHY MUST WE WAIT TO ACKNOWLEDGE LOVE?

"The living always believe they have more time, until time itself becomes the lesson."- *Santiago Dagon*

Why do we wait to say the words that matter most? We stand beside the people we love and hold back, as if affection were a currency that must be saved for later. We nod instead of embrace. We say take care instead of I need you. We choose composure over truth, and then one day, time withdraws the option to speak.

It is a quiet failing in the human heart, this belief that love can wait. We treat it as something renewable, as if each sunrise guarantees another chance to be kind. Yet love is not stored for later. It is perishable. It asks to be spoken in the moment, imperfectly, awkwardly, without rehearsal.

We wait because honesty frightens us. We fear that tenderness will expose us, that it will make us small in a world obsessed with appearing unbreakable. We wait for courage, for the right mood, for the apology to feel easier. But love does not need our timing; it needs our truth.

"Love is not measured in eloquence," Santiago wrote. **"It lives in the willingness to be seen."**

We let days pass like folded letters never sent. The father dies before the son can say I understand you. The friend moves away before we can whisper you mattered more than I showed. The mother's hands grow frail before the daughter can say I forgive you. And then we are left speaking to the air, asking forgiveness from the silence that remains.

Regret does not come from losing love. It comes from starving it. From withholding it out of pride, or distraction, or fear that it will not be returned. But love never needed to be perfect to be real. It only needed to be spoken while there was still breath to hear it.

We call it weakness to admit our care, yet it is strength. It is harder to stay open than it is to stay quiet. To tell someone you love them before the world demands it is to resist the small death of indifference.

We must stop waiting for the right moment. There is no perfect hour, no clear signal, no guarantee that tomorrow will be kind enough to let us finish our sentences. Speak now while the light still touches the faces you cherish.

Tell your father that he did enough. Tell your mother that her worry was love. Tell your son that his effort matters more than his mistakes. Tell your daughter that she is already enough. Tell your brothers, sisters, and friends you miss them. Tell yourself that softness is not a flaw.

"Love unspoken is a seed unwatered," Santiago Dagon wrote. **"It waits, but it cannot bloom."**

The bloom must happen in the present, in the unguarded hour when truth trembles but still steps forward. Gratitude before the eulogy. Apology before the distance. I love you before the door closes.

Because one day the room will grow quiet. And when it does, only the words we spoke will keep breathing.

So before this day ends, ask yourself, who have I not thanked? Who have I not forgiven? Who still waits to be told that they matter?

Do not let time become your teacher. Let presence be. Do not save your tenderness for funerals. Spend it wildly, now, while the people you love can still return it with their eyes, their hands, their living breath.

When your own dusk arrives, may they remember you not for restraint, but for courage. Not for your silence, but for the words you dared to give while the light was still warm on your face.

"The greatest tragedy," Santiago Dagon wrote, **"is not that we die, but that we wait too long to live truthfully in love."**

Nicholas J. Matyas

ACKNOWLEDGMENTS

To every father and son who have carried love without words, this book belongs to you. It was written not as an answer, but as a bridge, built from the same silence that once stood between us all.

For the fathers who learned to love through labor and responsibility, who believed that strength meant restraint, and for the sons who mistook that restraint for indifference, your story lives here. The quiet between you is not emptiness. It is the unspoken language of effort, waiting to be translated back into tenderness.

To the men who never found the courage to say what they felt, and to those who are finally finding it late in life, your timing is not too late. The heart does not keep a calendar. Every word spoken now still matters. Every act of presence still counts.

To the sons who waited for approval that never came, and to the fathers who wanted to say I am proud of you but didn't know how, you were both reaching for each other in the only ways you could. Love is never lost; it simply learns to travel by quieter roads.

This book exists because of you. Because somewhere in every generation, two voices keep trying to meet across the distance. One voice is weary, one restless, both longing for the same simple truth: I love you, and I never stopped trying to show it.

To my own father: your steadiness, your patience, your silence, and your late grace built the foundation for everything here. I understand now that your quiet was not absence. It was devotion, disguised as endurance.

And to my sons who find themselves somewhere in these pages: May you learn to speak the words your father could not. May you learn to forgive the silence that shaped you. May you remember that strength is not an absence of emotion, but the courage to feel without fear.

In the end, love is not proven by perfection, but by presence. It survives by the willingness to stay, to listen, and to begin again.

"In the end," Santiago Dagon wrote, **"love asks for nothing but presence. And presence is the only gift we truly leave behind."**

Nicholas J Matyas

ABOUT THE AUTHOR

NICHOLAS J. MATYAS

Nicholas J. Matyas is an American writer, educator, and personal development consultant whose work bridges reflection, faith, and the quiet search for meaning. His writing explores the meeting place between the seen and unseen, the ordinary and the eternal. Through his stories, he invites readers to pause, to listen, and to remember the sacred in everyday life. His work is not written from distance, but from experience: the long road between a father's restraint and a son's awakening.

As a son, he learned that love could live for decades without saying its name. As a father, he discovered that love, once spoken, becomes an act of courage. Through *When Love Learns the Way Back Home*, he gives voice to both. A voice to the generation that built through endurance, and to the generation that searches for meaning in that endurance. And, to differences between all generations Silent, Boomers, X, Millennial, Z, and Alpha, may they mend what we were not taught.

Nicholas is the founder of **Discovery Walkabout Press**, a creative home for works that explore humanity's interior landscapes: love, forgiveness, aging, and the quiet labor of becoming whole. His writing weaves lived emotion with the contemplative rhythm that defines his lifelong project: to help people listen to themselves, and to one another, without judgment.

Many of his books appear under two names: his own, and **Santiago Dagon**, the reflective pen voice through which timeless insight speaks. Santiago's words are not sermons, but echoes that serve as reminders that compassion often begins where language falters. Together, Nicholas and Santiago form a dialogue across time: the human and the spiritual, the personal and the universal.

Nicholas believes that storytelling, when honest, becomes a quiet kind of light, not to blind, but to guide. Each sentence is a small act of return, an invitation to listen, to forgive, and to begin again.

"Stories do not end when the book closes," Santiago Dagon wrote. **"They continue in the hearts that needed them most."**

To follow our ongoing works, visit Discovery Walkabout Press https://discoverywalkabout.com.

DISCOVERY WALKABOUT PRESS

Discovery Walkabout Press was founded on a simple belief: that reflection is not withdrawal from life, but a deeper way of living it. Its mission is to create media that nurture awareness, emotional intelligence, and intergenerational understanding. Media, in the form of books, articles, reflective guides, modern parables, contemplative workbooks and seminars that help readers rediscover peace, purpose, curiosity and live more consciously, love more gently, and see the extraordinary within the ordinary within themselves and the world around them.

Each title published under Discovery Walkabout Press follows a quiet philosophy: learning begins in stillness, wisdom grows through connection, and creativity flourishes when the mind is calm. The Press supports projects that bridge the spiritual and the practical, inviting readers to walk slowly through their own questions rather than rush toward answers.

At its heart, Discovery Walkabout Press stands for mindful storytelling, a journey of self-discovery, compassion, and clarity across generations.

As a publishing house and creative development studio we invite new and existing authors to grow together with us. Please reach out and contact us.

"We do not find truth by running faster. We find it by learning how to walk with wonder." - *Santiago Dagon*

www.ingramcontent.com/pod-product-compliance
Lightning Source LLC
Chambersburg PA
CBHW050826260726
48660CB00004B/1624